VIA AMAZON.COM
    8.00
+ 3.99 SH
   15.99
JUNE 2007

WAITING OUT A WAR

WAITING OUT
A WAR

The Exile of
Private John Picciano

Lucinda Franks

Coward, McCann & Geoghegan, Inc.
New York

For Lorraine and Thomas Franks

Contents

Introduction

One of the very first people to desert the U.S. Army in the Vietnam War years was a young man named John Picciano. When I met him three years ago, he was sitting in a small apartment in Uppsala, Sweden, surrounded by his books, the latest copies of *Time* and *Newsweek,* and a bundle of notes he had made during his years of exile. He had a story to tell. It was also the story of the tens of thousands of men who were the other casualties of America's longest war.

As many American men were exiled during this war as were killed in it.

The seeds of this book began back in the late fall of 1970. I was stationed in London for United Press International, and H. Roger Tatarian, who was then the editor of UPI, decided that I should make a trip to Sweden to take a look at the community of deserters that had been coming into the country at a high rate since 1968. There were only about 700 to 800 deserters in Sweden, but the community (and its problems) was very different from the much larger population of war resisters that had flooded into Canada. Whereas the majority of the exiles in Canada at that point were draft dodgers, nearly all those in Sweden were deserters—indeed, Sweden for a time was the only haven for refugees from the U.S. armed forces.

I met dozens of deserters scattered across Sweden. They were an intriguing, eclectic group. Each one had had a different experience growing up in postwar America, in confronting the military, and in taking flight from their homeland. There was, however, a certain common thread to their lives. I found one deserter who seemed to be fairly representative of the type of young man who was being trained for combat in Vietnam. John Picciano was born in an industrial town of working-class immigrant parents. Like a great many deserters, he never got to Indochina. He deserted before he could be sent there. Although his time in the service was brief, it was intense and overwhelming to him; it brought into focus his rather dreary, frustrating experience as an adolescent. In one sense, John's military experience was an exaggeration of all that came before and the trigger which made him desert not just the American Army, but the American way of life as he knew it.

I interviewed John and other members of the American deserters' community over a period of several weeks. Across the Atlantic, my colleague Peter Freiberg, based in New York, set out to interview John's family, friends, and old teachers in Lodi, New Jersey. In early 1971 I went to New York, and Peter and I collaborated in producing a 10,000-word five-part series of UPI articles which appeared in some 200 or more newspapers around the world.

Later Peter resumed regular assignments with UPI in

New York, and I took a leave of absence to pursue the story of the deserters. In November, 1971, I returned to Sweden for six weeks, to talk further with John. We had long and intensive interviews and I accompanied him here and there, observing as he carried on his daily life as an American refugee in Sweden. I spent many hours with his friends and a cross section of other deserters, as well as Swedish supporters, in Stockholm and Uppsala, immersing myself in their life-style wherever possible, following them on demonstrations and sitting in on meetings. Later I returned to the States for further conversations with the elder Piccianos, the friends John had left behind, amnesty groups, and returned exiles.

Each person I interviewed in Lodi and in Sweden carefully reconstructed the past, re-creating incidents and highlights of their experience. In most cases, I verified each incident which was related to me with one or more sources in order to piece together the story of John's life and the history of the American deserters' community as accurately as possible.

During the following two years, I undertook other projects and continued work on the book, keeping in contact with John through letters and telephone conversations. The finished product came into being not long after the United States halted the bombing of Cambodia, ending once and for all direct military involvement in Indochina. Much has changed since this book was first conceived. Support for the U.S. role in Vietnam steadily declined; we got out, and with the pullout of the troops went public interest in all aspects of the war. Watergate and related White House scandals have grabbed the headlines. Vietnam is history for most Americans. For at least 50,000 deserters and draft resisters living underground or in exile, however, the war still goes on. Nothing has changed for them. They still wait, as they have waited for years, to come home. They are perhaps the last piece of unfinished business of the American involvement in Vietnam—a problem that refuses to go away.

This book is an attempt to tell their story through the reconstruction of one man's life, told partly through his eyes and partly through the eyes of the journalist. The names and the characters are real except for two cases where the names of individuals who played fleeting roles in John's early life have been changed. The backgrounds of prominently featured deserters were checked against Department of Defense records.

This book would have been a very different book had it not been for the patient help of Roger Neville Williams, whose brilliant insights into the dilemma of the exiles helped to give the writer a deeper understanding of her subject. I would also like to extend my gratitude to Peter Freiberg for his diligent and thorough reporting and excellent sense of humor during the writing of the original UPI series, to George Carrano for his kind assistance in the early and final stages of the manuscript, and of course, to John Picciano, who was the reason for the book. Others who deserve thanks for their generous time and help are Rob Argento, Des Carragher, Jerry Condon, Barry Winningham, Father Thomas Hayes, and Bjorn Hoeijer.

LUCINDA FRANKS

New York City
December, 1973

Prologue

The wind swept strong and chill across the fields of McGuire Air Force Base. John was walking with it, walking so quickly his feet hardly touched the ground. The smell of the air was strong and the sky was black and open.

The barracks at Fort Dix were getting smaller, wavering in the bright moonlight. The nights had been the worst there. It had all come down on him then. The voices yelling "Kill! Kill!" The bayonets flying. Straw men collapsing. The fields filling with blood.

It didn't seem to matter where he was going. He could think about that later. What mattered now was the getting away. The Army was behind him, and whatever lay ahead, it could not be much worse.

1

After the War

On Sunday, October 26, 1947, an armored car proceeded down New York's Fifth Avenue drawing a caisson which bore the first soldier to return from the European war in a coffin. Across the river, in the bleak industrial town of Lodi, New Jersey, Constance Picciano gave birth to her first and only child, a son who was later to choose exile from his country rather than fight in one of its future wars.

Constance, a fragile and slight woman, had had a long and painful pregnancy, and the child John was a hard-won gift. After his birth, she was told that there could be no more. He was born into an exhausted world. There was the national sadness as the war dead who had been interred overseas were finally, with great ceremony, brought home for reburial and laid to ground in almost every city in the land. There was the spareness of living; if you wanted an automobile or refrigerator, you had to buy it secondhand, and there were still shortages of food and cigarettes.

There was also the euphoria of victory, the giddy optimism which follows the release from dull hardship. A time of unparalleled prosperity was just around the corner and who could say that a new and better world would not emerge from the terror and ruins of the old? America had saved Europe, and it was victorious and at one with itself.

The future held promise, that was certain, but it nevertheless appeared fraught with the unknown. The new world was settling into an uneasy mold. With the dawning of the superpowers, the United States took its place as one of the two imperial forces on the globe. The fight against fascism had taught America that the world was a dangerous place, that neighbors could not be trusted. The atomic bomb on Japan had provided a glimpse of what would happen should there be a third world war.

It seemed that perhaps an even more sinister power than Nazi Germany was gathering force and that America would have to shoulder a new burden. The Russians began to attack Truman, calling the Marshall Plan an imperialist conspiracy to make Europe the forty-ninth state, and the U.S. government did not take the harangues lightly. As the countries of Eastern Europe one by one came under the thumb of the Soviet Union, word of the red threat spread. Even Walt Disney, creator of animated fairy tales for children, announced that his Hollywood studios had fallen under the grip of a communist labor conspiracy.

A national fearfulness took seed as the country began to prepare for the Titanic struggle yet to come. Did it have enough alliances? Should it maintain large armed forces in Germany, England, Italy? Did it have enough arms, could it be first in the race for better weapons, satellites, ships, planes? There was a new sense of orthodoxy and conservatism. Some of the finest brains in the land were crystallizing into set patterns of thought, patterns which in years to come would form the basis for wars of untold consequence. As the cold war escalated, U.S. foreign policy became dominated by a single idea—winning out over the sinister forces behind the Iron Curtain.

If all the trends and emotional currents which went to make up the climate of postwar America affected Constance Picciano and her husband, John, it was only by osmosis. They lived in a small world, and they could tell you little about what went on in the outside one. They had more immediate things to think about. Like thousands of other war-weary Americans, the Piccianos threw themselves into the task of returning to normality. They were both in their early thirties and not particularly interested in traveling or having gay times or even in making more money than they needed. They remembered the Depression of the thirties, and the hardships of the past few years were fresh in their minds. When they met and married in 1946, more than anything else, they wanted security.

John Picciano, Sr., a heavyset man with big, kind eyes, a diffident manner, and a close crew cut, had come to Lodi from Italy when he was a boy of nine. His parents had left their goat farm in the province of Campobasso—northwest of Naples—in 1921 to share in the booming prosperity of the new world across the Atlantic. Old enough to remember the poverty and starkness of peasant life in Italy, John Sr. grew up devoted to his new homeland, where there were indoor toilets, electric lights, motorcars and movie houses, and a good meal every day of the week.

John Sr.'s father died several years after the family emigrated, and he was forced to leave high school and work in a factory to support his mother. The two carried on comfortably and soon bought a house just a few blocks off Lodi's main thoroughfare. The house on River Street was an odd house; it looked ordinary enough on the outside, with its red brick front, a tiny yard, and a tree which reached the second story; but once inside, you had to go to the basement to get to the kitchen, and the upstairs was reserved for paying guests in order to meet the mortgage. John loved the house, and as the man of the family, he spent his leisure moments learning carpentry to keep it in good repair.

Like most of the Italian immigrants who flooded into Lodi in the twenties, John Sr. assimilated quickly. The wild spirit of the twenties made it easy for the newcomers to join in the American way of life and feel as if they belonged. Women who had spent their girlhood farming became flappers, and the men sleeked down their hair after movie idol Rudolph Valentino. They danced the shimmy and the Charleston, argued passionately about the Dempsey fights, and formed baseball teams that made them famous throughout Bergen County.

In 1927, when Charles Lindbergh made history with his solo nonstop flight to Paris, Lodi exploded with patriotic pride. One would have thought their ancestors had fought in the Revolutionary War the way the citizens took to the streets, flags in hand, to cheer the "Lone Eagle"; like so many of them, he had made a pioneer journey across the Atlantic and provided proof that in America nobody had to be satisfied with dreams.

The people of Lodi worked for what they got. In 1926 workers at mills of the United Piece Dye Works, the town's main source of employment, went on strike for better wages and working conditions. For twelve months they picketed the mills. Some saw their families near starvation; others were beaten up and gassed before their demands were met. The strike received the attention of the entire American press and led to the organization of unions throughout the textile area of Bergen and Passaic counties.

In 1929 the Depression hit, and John Sr. and his mother, along with hundreds of others in the town, eventually lost their home. The day they moved out, John Sr. made himself a promise. Whatever else he did, he would get the house on River Street back. It was more than just a place to live; it had become the symbol of his family's new heritage, their small legacy as Americans.

During the Depression years, he worked nights and overtime on factory assembly lines, and in 1940 he bought back the house. In 1941, with America moving toward war, he tried to join the Army but was rejected on medical grounds, and so spent the war years working at home. In 1946 he took a wife and shortly afterward fathered a son. Having got most of the things he had wanted out of life, he settled down to enjoy them.

Constance Picciano was a frail, fluttery woman of Italian parentage much like her husband's. She was short and small-boned (John Sr. could rest his chin on her head) and moved about the house like a nervous squirrel. No one would have called her beautiful, but there was a certain attraction to her sharp features, pale skin, and black hair which, because of her scurrying, would lie in wispy disarrangement. She made a good home for her husband, keeping him satisfied with fine Italian cooking and a house that was always meticulously well ordered.

Constance did not take the prospect of motherhood lightly. During the long months of waiting, she often felt afraid, though of exactly what she did not know. She fidgeted and worried about the child growing inside her, and when he was born, she worried all the more. It wasn't that he was an unhealthy baby—he was plump and insatiably curious—but he seemed to have inherited some of his mother's restlessness and perhaps, she thought, some of her fears.

He would crawl about the house, babbling incessantly, poking into corners, and getting stuck under chairs. He hated being forced to stay in one spot and, when barely a year old, learned to climb out of his carriage when Constance's head was turned.

John Sr. was working nights at the textile mills then, and during the day he slept. It was hard on Constance, for by nature, she was a solitary person, disinclined to join women's groups or surround herself with friends. It had never occurred to her to extend herself much beyond the family circle, so her husband's absence was doubly felt. She filled the gap with her son.

They were seldom apart. She wouldn't go marketing without him and she hugged him a great deal of the time. They spent hours in the small backyard and he learned to draw letters in the dirt and jump off the step into her arms. Until the time he entered school, she was the only playmate he had.

Constance was an inseparable part of the baby John; she was his nourishment when he was hungry and his lap warmth when he felt cold; she was his legs when he was too tired to climb the stairs and his hands when he wanted a toy off the shelf. He could not imagine life without her. His father was different. He was someone apart and John watched him closely, watched when he took out his box of tools and sanded a table or fiddled with a loose hinge.

It wasn't long before he began to imitate John Sr., taking things apart and putting them together again. One day, when he was six and his parents were absorbed in television, he got a sudden urge to leave the room. He tried the door, but it was locked and that made him angry. Instead of asking to be let out, he picked up a screwdriver from the toolbox and took apart the lock, piece by piece. It was not the last time he dismantled locks during his childhood: He disliked being cooped up—a feeling which was to assert itself many years later in an Army barracks.

The first six years of John's life were years of joy. He was in a play world where you dug holes to China and whirled around in circles until the ground shifted places with the sky. There were no ghosts, no bogeymen then, and all things, even large dogs, were friendly. If something did frighten him, it would be driven away by his mother, who was strong and warm and everywhere, like the sun. Each day there was something to look forward to, something to scramble out of bed for—maybe an ice-cream cone or maybe just a new smell or a new feel, like putting your hands in mud for the first time.

In 1953 he entered Roosevelt Elementary School and his child's world ended. School brought in a host of feelings he hardly knew existed. For the first time he was afraid and anxious, for the mother was not there and the teachers were cold and stern and they walked back and forth waving rulers at the front of the room, their heels clicking loudly on the linoleum. Missing her and thinking about her, he forgot to listen and then the heels would be standing next to his desk and the ruler would come smashing down on it and he would cry and the others would laugh. Sometimes he would run from the room and throw up.

In the morning he often woke shaking, but Constance

would always force him to go to school. At the end of the day he would run home, and although the school was only a street and a field away, it seemed like miles. Even being home now was not the same, because he knew the next morning he would have to leave it again.

Constance worried more and more as she saw John become quieter, less active, and more prone to sickness. She tried everything. She became more attentive, even oversolicitous; she dressed him more warmly; she even had his tonsils out. Nothing seemed to help.

As if in sympathy, or perhaps out of despair, Constance was often ill and bedridden during his childhood. He would come to her bed, and looking at her pale face, the skin drawn tight around her cheekbones, he would feel panicky. When he was smaller, death was something to laugh about, like when Humpty Dumpty fell into a million pieces. But this was different. He was afraid she would die and he dreamed about it. Then he would fall sick himself and roll back and forth and whimper "Ooh, I'm going to die, I'm going to die."

John Sr. tried to bring his son out of these moods, making a joke of his fears, but John was not to be humored. Throughout elementary school, he remained subdued and introspective. At times he seemed to be brooding about something, as though a part of his mind had grown up much faster than his body, leaving innocence behind.

The Piccianos made a habit of taking periodic outings to visit relatives in the Bronx, across the river in New York. John was never very pleased on these occasions, for he liked to know that home was not far away. He became uneasy while traveling, and if, by chance, they boarded the wrong bus, he would be huffed for hours. The fact that some ten years later he rode countless buses, trains, and

boats to get as far away as possible from the base of security
that was so important to him as a child has been a source of
surprise to everyone who knew him well.

Making friends did not come easily to John and he spent
the hours of his boyhood in solitary pursuits. He liked to
put together little puzzles and he would refuse to go to bed
until he had fitted in every last piece. As he grew older, he
developed a practical streak and a distaste for playing
games for their own sake. One day when he was nine, his
parents found his erector set stuffed in the waste basket,
abandoned because he could build nothing "real" out of it.

So John Sr. taught his son carpentry. The two were
soon hammering and sawing together. They did repairs on
the porch and built a flagstone walk up the front of the
house. John was always making something—out of wood,
metal, or anything else he could get his hands on—and he
refurnished his parents' living room with a bookcase and
oak tables. Sometimes when he was supposed to be in
school, neighbors would see him, hammer in hand, furtively making his way through back streets toward the
lumberyard or the scrap pile.

He acquired an exacting attitude toward his work and
would become frustrated when things weren't perfect. He
once spent six hours trying to make the edge on a handmade table smooth with a small chisel, sweating angrily
because he did not have a plane.

As John grew to know his father, he moved away from
his mother. As a child, he had wished only to be closer and
closer to her, but now that he had to leave childhood
behind, he wanted only to shake her off. Like all mothers
when their one son begins the struggle toward independence, Constance followed his moves with a critical and
overinterested eye.

She fussed over him and she nagged. Where were his dirty socks, why didn't he put them in the hamper, where was he this afternoon, and if he was only over there, why couldn't she see him when she looked down the road? . . . If he didn't eat up those eggs, his hair would probably fall out. The two bickered much of the time, but they seldom had battles that were not forgotten the next day and their basic hold on each other remained intact.

Before he left elementary school, John had found one close friend—Ken Barry, a shy sensitive boy who lived just a block away. Ken, like John, was a loner and the two gravitated toward each other because of their love of science and their mutual hatred of after-school sports.

To avoid the trauma of watching the town fill up with football crowds, they would head for New York on Saturdays to while away their time at the Natural History Museum. On summer nights, when other boys were trading baseball cards on back porches, Ken and John would study the stars through John's telescope.

Every Sunday the boys went together to mass at St. Joseph's Roman Catholic Church—not that they could have told you why. They never thought or talked about religion the way they did about science; they just accepted it as part of life, like washing the family car on Saturday.

By the time Ken and John finished eighth grade and started off to high school the town of Lodi had begun to depress them. It was only a few miles from New York City and Paterson, New Jersey, but to them, it could have been in the middle of the Sahara. There was a boys' club and a movie house, but not much else for the young. It was a place of pizza parlors, bowling alleys, and corner bars. The paper and textile factories, with their belching smokestacks, seemed to dominate the town. More often than not, the air was gray, and even when the sun burned, a faint grime would seem to creep back through the streets with a nudging relentlessness.

It was, however, a close-knit town—the kind where the police chief, the county clerk, and the high school English teacher might well have been cousins. For those who belonged, and for those who did not, it was a place of warmth and hospitality; families like the Piccianos suffered no hostility for preferring to keep to themselves.

It wasn't unusual for the town's schoolteachers to have taught the fathers and uncles of their pupils. Once settled, people seldom left Lodi. Indeed, there wasn't much need to venture far from the town, since most of the residents found work in its factories. Nor did there seem to be any reason for them to depart from the way of life established by their immigrant parents. Things were done in the old way. Learning was gotten from the book, and the church and government were absolutes not to be questioned.

Patriotism and town pride run high in Lodi. The older folk still talk of the time "former President Theodore Roosevelt" came on a campaign visit and the town declared a holiday. They remember being children during World War I, buying war stamps and collecting peach pits used to make an antigas chemical for the trenches. Others boast of the crack civil defense which Lodi organized during World War II and the 1,800 men it gave to the armed services. There is no shortage of volunteer bartenders at Lodi's American Legion bar and the men schoolteachers tend to gravitate to the Veterans of Foreign Wars hall after classes to play pool or cards.

World War II changed Lodi, as it changed hundreds of small towns throughout the United States. After the years of deprivation, the consumer appetite exploded, and so did the economy. Business expanded, wages climbed with profits, the population ballooned, and hamlets like Lodi grew into miniature cities. New industries settled into the town and housing developments went up. Stores either expanded and modernized or shut down.

The once open grounds which served as baseball fields and parks were invaded by factories and warehouses. Many of the little people—the small shopkeepers, the shoemakers, the bakers—were forced to sell out and take jobs on the assembly lines. As young boys, Ken and John watched as an Italian delicatessen and a bakery near their homes were razed and the grassy fields in back gouged out for urban renewal. By the time the boys were adults, the only thing which had been built on the dry rubble-encrusted land was a construction shed.

2
Coming Up for Air

The library was very still and smelled of leather and lemon oil. John stood between the stacks and listened. You could hear the pages of a book being turned it was so quiet, or the gentle flapping of a window shade. Those were good sounds, sounds he loved. They were sounds that let the dreams come easily.

It was not that the Lodi Public Library was a particularly romantic place. A squat brick building with good lighting and sturdy tables, it was constructed after World War II in memory of the town's fallen sons. As with most of the institutions in Lodi, its architects had utility rather than art in mind. The library's neutrality was what appealed to John. It was like a free zone, a place which offered refuge from all the things that made him feel like bursting open—boring classes, peckish parents, and in-and-out high school popularity games.

Getting to and from the free zone was costly, however.

He always felt vaguely ashamed about it. Being seen in the library after school instead of on the sports field or in Pap's luncheonette making it with the girls put you in a certain category. It identified you with the creeps, the twinks, the guys who had too many pimples or too many brains or voices that hadn't quite changed.

John felt uneasy about many things he liked to do. Perhaps that is why shortly after he entered Lodi High School in 1962 he began to develop a peculiar walk. He would shuffle, almost skate, across the library floor and disappear into the stacks, as though he imagined if he didn't actually lift his feet, no one would notice him.

Once in the stacks, however, he would relax. The sight of so many books excited him. He was interested in many subjects—history, science, politics, literature—and he read one book after another, spurred by an obscure sense that there would not be enough time for him to find out all he wanted to know. Although he imagined himself alone, the librarian, Paul Speziale, was always aware of his presence. Speziale, an English teacher who worked part time at the public library, was intrigued by the fact that John would sit hunched over a volume of H. G. Wells one day and *Great Movies of the 40's* the next, reading them both with equal absorption. There were few youngsters of high school age in Lodi who had such an appetite for collecting information.

Across from the library, several of John's peers had occupied a street corner. He looked out the window and studied them. They wore studded leather jackets and tough hostile faces, faces which had long ago lost the air of expectancy and anticipation found in the expressions of their more well-placed contemporaries in the suburbs.

They moved about in a pack, bodies loose, heads bobbing, and when they decided to light and take over a patch of territory—a corner café or a car park—they would not just stand around, they would position themselves as if modeling for the cover of the *Saturday Evening Post*. Each would strike a different pose. Mack rotating his jaw around a wad of chewing gum. Bernard twirling his dog tag. Al drumming out the "Duke of Earl" on the bonnet of an old Chevrolet convertible. Gary taking the cigarette out from behind his ear and combing back the sides of his heavily oiled ducktail.

"Hey, Mack, wind up a Charlene Esposito doll and whaddya get?"

"Lotsa boobies and one big box!"

"She put out?"

"You gotta believe it. Lemme tell you about last Friday night. . . ."

The group went into a huddle. Another tale of sexual conquest on a star-drenched forty-ninth-yard line. John wondered how many of the stories the guys told were true. It was good if you could tell those stories about girls, the ones who wore tight Orlon sweaters. It was part of what made you belong. Like being able to remove the hubcaps from a car in less than thirty seconds, knowing to stuff your back pocket with Saran Wrap before a date, wearing your trousers snug, your shoes slightly pointed, and your shirt buttoned up just halfway. All those things had to come naturally to you to be what every guy wanted to be, and that was cool.

Cool. What *was* cool, anyway? He didn't exactly know. Standing on the corner tossing a nickel up and down. That was cool. Cool was slapping your knees in time with the jukebox or staring down a stranger or snapping your fingers in the face of an old lady. It was shooting a moon from the window of a broken-down painted-up Chevy.

One thing that was not cool was John Picciano. He

would never have the nerve to snap his fingers at old ladies and he could seldom bring off giving someone the hairy eyeball. He caught sight of his reflection in the window and appraised his looks harshly. He was too heavy to wear his trousers tight. No matter which way he turned or squinted to blur the image, it looked to him as though he had swallowed a small melon, and when he slouched, you could see the spread of his navel through his T-shirt. He was actually not considered by others to be bad-looking. His hair was thick and dark, and he had fine large hands and a waggish smile which took people by surprise. He tended to ignore these facts, however, and developed the sloppy habits of one who thinks it is expected of him. His shirt often hung out in the back and there was a period where it did not seem to matter to him whether he but-toned his cuffs or not.

It was in the solitude of the library that John would think over embarrassing moments. One time he thought about a recent school sock hop he had been to, and winced. He usually skipped those dances, but he had wanted to go to this one. He had wanted very badly to meet some girls, because his luck with girls had been dismal. He was stiff and shy, and mostly he would just stand in the parking lot after school and watch them pass. Occasionally he would muster up the courage to say something to one, but if she said something back, he would be at a loss. If she said "hi," his jaw would lock and he'd look around distraughtly as if to ask someone, What do I do next? He had become known as "the big mover" at dances because he would go down the line of girls, starting with the most beautiful, and when he had come to the last "no," he would go outside the gym and have a cigarette. Once, however, it was different and a beautiful girl had accepted, and then suddenly he had fifteen other girls around him. All evening he did the twist and the gravy and the soupy shuffle.

He thought maybe the same thing would happen again, so for the next sock hop he went out and bought a hi-roll shirt and had it monogrammed. A bunch of the guys, including Dan and Chickie Cucuo, twins who lived down the street, were going to pick him up. When they arrived, they took one look at him and went into a seizure of hoots.

"Hey, John, where you coming, you're not coming with us," one of the guys said. They were all in open-necked shirts. "You make us look bad."

So John went back into the house and spent the evening watching TV.

Later, after the dance, the Cucuos came round and told him it had been meant as a joke. "You take things too serious," they said.

John's friends spent a lot of time with him trying to make him more hip for, in spite of the fact that he really didn't fit in at all—he walked funny, wore square clothes, didn't play sports—they kind of liked him. They didn't understand him, the way he'd take walks by himself and let little kids come up and smack him and not do anything about it. But you couldn't help liking John, and some people, although they wouldn't admit it, admired him. He was really a generous guy. He would always be lending out money, and when his parents bought him a car in his senior year, he let the Cucuos use it whenever they wanted and taught Chickie how to drive. He could be very deter-mined when he put his mind to something and he had a strange way of turning potentially uncool situations into triumphs. Like the time some of them had decided to climb the school fence to play cards on top of the fire escape. John, knowing he might not make it up, dashed home, got some tools, and had picked the gate lock by the time the rest of them had scaled the fence.

The Cucuo twins were exasperated when their attempts at making John fit in failed. He wanted to change, they said between themselves, but something seemed to be holding him back. How could a guy wear white socks and own only one suit—it was the same one, many times altered, that he had been confirmed in at age eleven—and expect to get by without being put down? He just never learned.

The fact was that John himself didn't know where he wanted to be. He didn't really want to be "out," but then he didn't really want to be "in." He didn't want to wear black socks (he felt cleaner in white), nor did he want to sever relations with his friend Sal Campanella. The guys had warned him if he kept associating with Sal he'd get a bad reputation. Sal had a noticeable lisp, and when he went by, the guys would sometimes whistle and wiggle their hips.

In the end, John struck an uneasy balance between the two. He drew away from Sal and Ken Barry, his old childhood friend and fellow loner, and he began to spend more time with the Cucuos and their friends. He got some sharper clothes, started cracking his knuckles, and he even learned how to make people laugh with him as well as at him. You couldn't help laughing with John, they said, because he was always making noises. Anything he could pick up—a sound or a few words, like "bop-she-bop-she-bop"—if it sounded good to him, he would say it over and over in goofy ways, and even if it wasn't funny to begin with, it would sound funny after a while.

Those were not the times when John felt best with himself, however. It was better when he was alone, idling by the Saddle River on a windy day watching the long bank grass part and repart or in the library reading about conquistadors and Mohicans. It wasn't that he enjoyed being alone. He just couldn't find many people to share his thoughts with, and some of his thoughts he was sure others would consider weird. Sometimes, for instance, he tried to imagine what it was like beyond the stars or he wondered how it would be if there was suddenly no pull of gravity and people started floating up off the ground. How could he explain thoughts like that to the Cucuos? He might get beaten up.

Such imaginings and meditations often met with scorn in Lodi, for like much of America in the fifties and early sixties, it had little use for anything that smacked of the intellectual. ("See that egghead? Color him Red!") Indeed, even the word itself was suspect in a climate where Joseph McCarthy was still a household name, if not a household hero, and communism threatened to end the reign of peace and prosperity that had followed the war. To bring up politics was socially verboten and to ask a man his religion was almost like inquiring whether he had been to bed with his mother.

With television in almost every home, it became less necessary to read, to think on things too hard, to wonder. It was less acceptable to express feelings, to show you were moved by something. What high schooler in 1962 would risk being accused of an open show of emotion? Who indeed would even admit to the fact that he felt one? Love was something that occurred on the Hit Parade; joy, a word used by grandmothers; and suffering, something that happened to cancer patients or the starving children of India. Anger was perhaps one of the few feelings that could be expressed, but even that had a collective quality about it; more often than not, it was a weapon that disappeared like bats and bicycle chains into the trash cans when the police came.

It was no time for the individual. Speaking out meant you rocked the boat. And to do that was to be different and to be different was to be, well, slightly un-American. If anyone doubted how strong America was engraved on the mind, not only as a country but as an idea, a way of life, one had only to look around. There were Miss America televisions by Philco, Young America crystal glassware by Libby, Americana kitchens, American Bandstand, Chevrolets to see the USA, and home-sized bonus flags made available by Mrs. Filbert's Margarine.

For John, the ubiquitous star-spangled banner had a special meaning. It might have been the only thing which prevented him from being expelled from school. Often, he felt an insuppresible urge to drift off in class and then he would fix his eyes on the flag which fluttered in a metal stand next to the open window, counting the stars first from the left, then from the right, down from the top, up from the bottom. It kept him awake (while the drone of the teacher's voice fought to put him to sleep) better than a pinch on the arm.

He always sat in the back of the room. Even history classes bored him. What had been so real and exciting when he read about it in the library—the wars, the brave conquests, the discoveries of new frontiers—seemed to evaporate in a cloud of dusty data in the classroom. He learned nothing that occupied his mind beyond the final bell, nothing that he could apply to his life outside the school gates. Nevertheless, he did his homework faithfully and memorized enough facts and figures to pass most of his tests, mostly out of fear of what would happen if he did not.

As far as the teachers at Lodi High School were concerned, John was an enigma. He fell into that category of "unreachables," boys who could or would not find a footing in the system. When they talked about him in the faculty lounge, which was seldom, they described him as an introvert who was a little too deep within himself. "I know he has a lot of potential," his English teacher Paul Speziale remarked once. "But it's like having a beautiful car and keeping it in the garage. If you don't use it, what good is it?" The faculty did not worry or bother much about John. He was passing his courses and got good citizenship marks. As long as they could keep boys like him on the straight and narrow and teach them enough to be useful members of the community, they would have done their job.

Constance Picciano insisted that her son not miss a day of school, even when he complained of feeling unwell. She and her husband did not want anything out of the ordinary for him—indeed they were impatient with his constant talk of being "somebody"—but they wanted him to have something better than they had had. It was important to them that he get the high school diploma that John Sr. had never been able to get, that he have the things other kids had—decent clothes, plenty of pocket money, a car before he graduated—that eventually he find a nice girl and learn a skilled trade which would give him security for the rest of his life.

So when he came home one day lugging a carton containing a secondhand 1929 *Encyclopaedia Britannica* set, they were caught up short. It had cost $64. "I don't believe it," his mother said over and over. "You save up sixty-four dollars and you spend it on what. An outdated encyclopedia!" His father told him he could have just about bought Texas with that amount of money.

John tried to argue with them. "Look, sometimes I need a piece of information. I need to know something and I've got to have an encyclopedia," he said.

"For what," said his mother. "What do you need to know that you can't learn at school?"

Sometimes, the Piccianos did not understand their only child. These were the greatest years ever, great prosperous days after the war. He should be out having fun like other kids. He should put his money in a bank account, save up for a car to take the girls around in instead of blowing it on encyclopedias. He'd better have his fun now, they warned, because he wouldn't be able to have it when he grew up.

Adulthood, in the experience of the Piccianos, was a long plodding pursuit of stability and permanence. Once these plateaus had been reached, struggle and the drive for betterment ceased as a way of life. It was enough jealously to guard the basic comforts which had taken so long to acquire. Thus, the Piccianos and other immigrants to America tended to be on the lookout for anything which threatened to disturb their hard-won security. Excesses of any kind—heavy drinking, too much talking, too much thinking—were discouraged. They took things as they came, and as long as most of what came their way was foreseeable, they were satisfied. John Sr., for instance, would never think of tying one on at Kelsey's bar down the road. His life was governed by habit and he would come home after work every day at about ten minutes on either side of five o'clock.

People in Lodi tended not to measure how happy they were or how much good luck a day had brought them, but rather how much unpleasantness they had been able to avoid. They were inclined to converse in negatives like: "How you today, Nick?" "Oh, not too bad and you?"

"The same. How's the kid?" "He's OK. Hasn't got into too much trouble."

The circle which people drew around their lives was small. They knew nothing of backyard barbecues, bridge luncheons, and hospital aid balls where silk brushed against crushed velvet and the laughter rang shrill and throaty. That kind of life belonged to the other half of America across the river in Bronxville or Manhattan. The Piccianos spent their weekends in quieter ways. A night out for them was a night in the home of a friend, the men drinking Rheingold around the *Perry Como Show* and the women sitting in the kitchen in pinafore aprons chatting about how Cousin Donna got a Maytag when she married.

As John grew older, the monotony of life in Lodi began to affect him. He felt a restlessness growing inside him and that restlessness made him read more and more on his own—not to escape the world, as he had done previously, but to seek answers to questions bothering him.

Orwell's *Animal Farm* started him on a new course of thinking. One of the book's themes—that all animals are equal but some are more equal than others—teased his mind. Equality. Equality and freedom. He had never really thought about what those words meant. He could not say he really understood them. His mind seemed to stick on the word "freedom" (it had a brave, towering ring) and he tried to imagine how it applied to his own life.

He lived in a free country. He had heard that phrase many times. It was the freest country in the world. There were no knocks on the door at 3 A.M. and a man could go as high as he wanted and communism would never be allowed to threaten that right. But what exactly did it mean to be free? He was free to come and go, free to buy a soda, take a nap, build a table, read a book when he pleased.

Those were things which were easy to define, but he felt there was another kind of freedom, something that he could not quite put his finger on. He half perceived that he had been deprived somewhere along the way. It had something to do with the fact that he felt guilty about buying the $64 encyclopedia, that his teachers treated him like a child who had to be kept in line, that he seemed to be utterly alone in those intense indefinable longings for which he could find no expression. He harbored the suspicion that what he wanted to be was very different from what he was "free" to be.

John read books on socialism, on economics, on twentieth-century history. He was as fascinated by *The Rise and Fall of the Third Reich* and the growth of Nazism as he was by Roosevelt and the New Deal. He was, in fact, engrossed by any figure who was able to change the course of events—perhaps because of the resistance to change which he saw in the atmosphere of his hometown. For the first time he found a class at school—American history—in which he felt a part; he spoke out regularly and was a leader in some lively class debates.

In studying the lives of great men like Roosevelt, he came to realize that he would never be content doing the kind of work his father did. Clocking into the factory each morning, clocking out again at night. He thought of himself at the age of seventy-five. Would he be sitting in a nameless boardinghouse, toothless, bloodless, fading off into an anonymous death? That thought made him cringe. He wanted something more. He wanted to add something to something, to be recognized as a man who mattered.

The Piccianos distrusted these stirrings in John. "What can come of so much dreaming?" said his father. "It doesn't put food on the table." He would have liked his son to think about being a carpenter, good honest work where he could use his hands. "You don't have to read books to be a big shot," he said. "We all end up the same, you know."

By the time John entered his last year of high school the boredom and frustration which he kept inside for so long had gradually turned outward into anger. He came out of his isolation and developed a cocky don't give a damn attitude. Two events helped to give him confidence: He acquired a used white Ford (a proud gift from his parents) and the beginnings of a heavy beard which made him appear older than his age. His friends looked at him with a new respect when they found he could pass for twenty-one in a liquor store. Even his mother said to him one day, "John, you've changed. You act like you know a lot."

Deciding that high school was a joke and that he was a lot smarter than any of his teachers, he began to challenge them. His first target was the school librarian, Miss Gertrude LaVow, with whom he had never got along. She was a strict woman with silver hair and a straight back, and it seemed to John that she was much less concerned with books than with dirty drawings. She would sit on a high stool by the card catalogue, her eyes roaming over the tables full of students. Occasionally she would walk up and down peering over shoulders, and if she caught a boy scribbling a lewd picture, she would clamp her hands on his shoulder, steer him into the corner, and give him a long lecture.

John and his friends had worked out a daily routine to bait her. They would clear their throats loudly, drop books, or make obscene noises, falling quickly silent as soon as she looked up. One day they dared John to kick over her stool. To everyone's surprise, he walked over picked it up, and brought it down to the floor with a crash.

Miss LaVow banned him from the library for several weeks.

After that, making trouble came easy to John. During a history exam, he staged a performance that earned him the respect of even the most apple-polishing of his classmates. He had studied hard for the exam and finished well before time was up. He had to go to the toilet, however, so he brought his exam paper up to the proctor, a woman, and asked to be excused. She refused, insisting that the rules did not allow him to leave before the others were finished. He argued. She was adamant. Their voices got louder and John got angrier. Finally, he tore his exam in two and walked out of the room. "Shove it up your ass," he shouted as he went.

Such behavior had the inevitable effect on his citizenship marks as well as his academic average. For a while, he was in a precarious scholastic position, but by the time graduation came he had managed to get his marks up to a B–C average, high enough so that he could risk once again expressing his newfound aggressiveness.

Practice sessions for the graduating ceremony were annoying him. Jerry Tamburello, the faculty director of student activities, drilled the class over and over with an eye to making the procession go off with a military precision. He lined them up according to height and had them parade down the aisle for five days after school, thumping straight the odd back, and constantly rearranging arms until he decided they should march with one arm to the side and the other bent out in a style reminiscent of Napoleon. If the line became crooked, he would scream, "Stop!" and shut off the record player and start the procession over again.

John decided he would boycott the dress rehearsal. He

stood in the shadows at the back of the hall and watched as the seating arrangement fell into chaos because of his absence. When Tamburello realized that each boy was receiving the diploma of the person ahead of him, he halted the rehearsal.

"Where's Picciano?" he roared.

"Here, sir," said John, grinning from the back.

"Get up here! What do you think you're doing?"

"Mail me my diploma," yelled John and walked out.

John had intended to stay away from graduation as a symbolic protest against the school system, but his mother foiled the plan. As in the past, when reason, argument, and threats failed, she appealed to his filial instincts as a last resort. Accusing him of driving her to an early grave, she cried, complained of stomach cramps, and went to bed until he gave in and agreed to receive his diploma with the others.

Soon after graduation, John decided to stop being a practicing Roman Catholic. Although his values and code of ethics were only half-formed, it was important to him to act on principle whenever he encountered something he sensed was not quite right. He had become increasingly disillusioned with mass at St. Joseph's Church, which he had attended regularly with his parents since childhood. The Scripture readings seemed to travel past his ear like the sound of water in a brook, melodic and soothing but incoherent. He had tried to concentrate, to understand what the words meant, but each time he digested a phrase it would fly from his mind, never to return. Once he had fallen asleep in mass and another time, in confession, he had had trouble keeping a straight face when the priest asked him if he had any sexual sins to admit. When that same priest told him that there were certain exceptions to the commandment "Thou shalt not kill," war being one of them, John decided that the church was a house of men rather than the house of God.

Few of John's classmates knew what they wanted to do after they graduated in June, 1966. There were not many who had applied to college, as it was not generally expected of them, and most thought in terms of getting a job and making their homes in Lodi. John Picciano knew only what he did *not* want to do. He knew he had to leave Lodi, but he also realized how difficult it would be to resist the temptation of falling into the slow, familiar, easy way of the town. It was a warm, safe existence. He knew the faces he would meet when he walked down River Street in the morning. He knew there would be ravioli or pot roast on the table at night. His childhood fear of traveling from home was still alive; he hated to leave this life even for a day, but at the same time he had a continual feeling of suffocation, as though he were swimming underwater and could not hold his breath much longer.

When he turned eighteen, John registered for the draft as required, although he was less than enthusiastic about the prospect of joining the Army. He had wanted to go to college—his rank in the top half of his class was good enough to gain him admission to a state university—but his parents, their resources drained by family illness, were unable to afford four years of tuition and expenses. So he decided to spend the summer job hunting.

He had always loved woodworking and he tried first to get a job as a carpenter's apprentice. However, the labor boom caused by the coming of age of the World War II "war babies" combined with the fact that he was healthy and draftable made it difficult to get any work at all. He tried employer after employer, applying for jobs in stores, factories, offices. It was the same everywhere. As soon as they found out he was "draft bait," the interview ended abruptly with the explanation that the company wanted someone on a permanent basis. "Come back and see us when you get this draft thing out of the way," was the usual reply.

John became bitter. He felt as if he was wearing a 1-A on his forehead like a scarlet letter. The more he thought about it, the more it struck him as ironically unjust; because he was of draft age, he was being penalized by the very companies and businesses which he soon might be called to defend.

With no job and a lot of spare time on his hands, John began informing himself about the war in South Vietnam which was even now indirectly affecting his life. In the past, he had paid little attention to current events. The election of John F. Kennedy to the Presidency, which had excited so many middle- and upper-middle-class young people, had had little effect on John and his friends. But now, as the Johnson administration escalated U.S. involvement in Southeast Asia, national politics and the burgeoning controversy over the war engaged the attention of even the smallest of America's newspapers. John followed the daily dispatches on the progress of the conflict. He read Lederer and Burdick's *The Ugly American* and tried to apply it to what was happening in Vietnam. He considered the possibility that the United States was making a mistake by intervening in what Johnson's critics were insisting was a civil war, the possibility that by trying so hard to stop underdeveloped countries from going toward communism we were actually forcing them there.

After a few months of idleness, John finally resorted to taking a job hauling furniture at a mail-order firm warehouse near his home. It was easy to get work there. Low wages and poor working conditions produced a constant labor turnover. The warehouse had no windows, poor lighting and was musty and airless. It had stood there as long as anyone could remember and the stairs were tiny and narrow as though, it seemed to John, they had been constructed in the days of child labor. Most of the employees went around shirtless because of the heat, and after two people fainted one hot afternoon, the management put out a supply of salt pills.

Working there was not very pleasant, but at least it was a job. John slowly found out that it was also an education. The work force was made up almost entirely of blacks and poor people who were on welfare at least as often as they were working. John had never been exposed to this class of have-nots before, nor had he been aware of how differently the system treated such people.

There was no union to protect the workers; people were dismissed arbitrarily at what often seemed to John to be merely the whim of the management. A black man whom he had become friendly with, for instance, was fired on the grounds of "irresponsibility" because the firm had got wind of the fact that he was heavily in debt although he had never missed a day of work.

At the end of nine months, John had had enough of the warehouse. A chance meeting with the manager persuaded him to quit. He and a fellow worker had been told to remove an air-conditioning unit from his office and install a larger one. The pair hauled the unit upstairs in sweltering heat and entered the office, which was cool and airy in contrast with the rest of the building. The manager, a pudgy, balding man, looked up at them with distaste when they asked him to move so they could hook up the new unit. Afterward he told them to take the old one out by way of the fire escape so their work clothes would not "offend the customers on the floor level."

The fire escape was steep and rickety. The two made it down the first few steps balancing their heavy load rather precariously but then John's colleague, who was on top, suddenly slipped. The air conditioner fell, bounced off John's foot, and thudded to the ground. John let out a howl and the manager ran to the window. When he saw what had happened, he swore and said the cost of the shattered unit would be taken out of their salaries.

John quit the mail order warehouse and sat home for several days nursing his injured foot. He became depressed. It was as though he had driven the wrong way up a one-way street; no matter what he did, he seemed to collide with the rest of the world. He brooded over the fact that he and his friends, average guys who were not brilliant but not dumb either, were having such a hard time finding jobs. There seemed to be no opportunities open to him, nobody who was willing to give him a chance.

Nobody, that is, except the U.S. Army. It was the summer of 1967 and draft calls were reaching a peak. With his friends being inducted right and left, John's mind turned once again to thoughts of the military, of Vietnam. He knew he had to try to make some kind of sense out of the conflicting interpretations of this remote war. He read Bernard Fall on the history of Vietnam and the long struggle of the people there to be free of foreign domination. He wondered how the Vietnamese peasant felt. Did he know anything about the world beyond his home, his family, his farm? Did he know the difference between communism and capitalism? What did he think when all those foreign tanks came riding over his crops and the jets strafed and bombed his fields?

John had heard fantastic stories about the war from

Vietnam veterans in Lodi, and he wondered which of them were true. "You wouldn't believe it, you just won't believe what goes on over there," one old school acquaintance kept saying. He told of bulldozing and setting fire to South Vietnamese villages, of three and four generations of families who refused to leave their homes, who ran out finally amid the smoke and flames like ants, of Vietcong prisoners pushed out of helicopters, of the tortures of other prisoners and the *carte blanche* the soldiers had in trying to extract information from the captured suspects ("Do anything to them, just so long as it doesn't leave marks"). The friend would avoid passing construction sites where old buildings were being torn down; it made him break out in a sweat and become short of breath.

Others were proud of having served in Vietnam, proud of the bronze stars they came home with. One fellow would boast about the number of Cong he'd killed. The Vietnamese were animals, he said; they lived in dirty huts, wore pajamas, never bathed, and they had killed a couple of his buddies, leaving them to die slowly in the heat from maggot-infested wounds. After that, he had cut off the ears of every Vietcong he killed, he said.

Eisenhower's famous statement on the war—that if general elections were held in South Vietnam, 80 percent of the people would vote communist—left an impression on John. Being of a generation which did not remember the McCarthy era and the anti-communist paranoia which had so influenced the thinking of his elders, he could not fully understand why it would be so devastating for the United States to allow a country like Vietnam to have the kind of government which the majority of its population apparently wanted.

He wondered what was so evil about socialism and

communism and he questioned whether the system of government in his own country was necessarily the best. The system seemed, after all, to exclude him from its acclaimed benefits and appeared to favor the rich and the educated; if nothing else, his own experience as unemployable "draft bait" had taught him something about the system.

Such thoughts had been steeping in John's mind for several days when he received a letter ordering him to take his preinduction physical. It caught him unawares. Indeed, he was hardly awake when he gathered with the other youths in the predawn hours in front of his local draft board to await the bus which would ship them to the Army examining station. Their faces looked surreal in the half-light, gray-white, partly fearful, partly curious. There was the smell of hair tonic and teaberry gum . . . warm bread from the bakery next door . . . a blast of exhaust as the bus rolled up.

At the center, there was the endless waiting in lines, the mental test, the security clearance forms, and finally the physical. The examinees stood in rows at arm's length while the doctors moved up and down like assembly line workers, each one prodding and poking a different organ. It all began to run together in front of John's eyes. It was as though he was not really there but watching a silent movie, a blur of cold stethoscopes and sharp steel instruments, examiners whipping past in speeded-up motion, clerks at their heels scribbling down the results. Kidneys, liver, spine, intestines. Eyes, mouth, ears, nose. Does everybody have one?

Somebody muttered, "It's the A-one ass inspector," and the motion stopped abruptly. A voice in the front yelled, "Drop your shorts," and John felt himself drop down from the waist with the rest of the naked dozens, awaiting the assault of a hemorrhoid-searching finger. Visions of Orwell's *Animal Farm* rushed with the blood to John's upside-down head.

I must be a dog, he thought, as he trotted abstractedly from room to room, leaving a cup of urine here, a vial of blood there. At the urine station, a physician was making a red-faced examinee give a second specimen in his presence because the first contained abnormal substances. *We all must be dogs,* thought John, *just pretending to be human beings, like pets who are pampered into thinking they are people.*

When he reached the third and final part of the examination, he thought with relief that it was almost over. His blood pressure, however, recorded high. The examining sergeant gave him a suspicious look and told him to sit down and remain quiet. The room was filled with men waiting for a second blood pressure test. Those with low counts were told to do jumping jacks.

An officer peeked in the door and asked why so many people were sitting around.

"Having trouble passing. A lot of funny business going on today," said the sergeant.

"They'll pass," said the officer curtly and disappeared.

A long-haired fellow examinee sitting next to John told him that a lot of draft boards were having trouble filling their quotas. "They're out to get everybody, and if you've popped some pills, forget it," he said. "They'll keep you here all week. If your blood pressure ain't right, they'll get it right."

John nodded as though he understood what the boy meant, but inwardly he tried to piece it all together. Throughout the day he had heard snatches of conversation about guys who were doing different things to "evade the draft"—taking drugs before the physical, feigning homosexuality, having braces installed. The most popular method was apparently getting the family doctor (or paying one) to write a letter certifying you were physically or psychiatrically unfit for service.

All this was new to John. While he had heard about the emerging draft resistance movement—the antiwar and antidraft demonstrations, the massive draft-card burning in New York City's Sheep Meadow that spring—it had not had any immediate impact on him. Like the love and drug culture which preceded it, the movement was started by and directed toward the children of the upper and middle classes. The draft-counseling boards which were springing up in university towns and big cities had not come to working-class boroughs like Lodi, New Jersey. Indeed, few of the youths in such towns, where the clinic or the city hospital often substituted for the family doctor, would have had access to a physician who would be willing to hype up an old knee injury or exaggerate a minor condition to get their patient out of the draft. As for other methods such as drugs, John would never have known to take Benzedrine to raise his blood pressure; the most he and his friends had ever done was sniff glue.

Although the hope that he would not pass the physical had idled in the back of John's mind, it had never occurred to him actively to seek to fail it. He had a history of occasional high blood pressure, and he supposed that could have gotten him off. But even if he had known how to go about getting a medical certificate attesting to the fact, he wondered whether he would have had the nerve to do it. Somehow, it didn't sit right. It seemed chicken. After all, he thought, they're going to get their quotas no matter what. If one person fakes out, that just means they'll take somebody else in his place.

As he left the examining center—his blood pressure having dropped into the normal zone after several hours of remaining almost stationary—it suddenly struck him that the somebody else was himself. Before, it had all seemed vaguely remote, something that might happen next month or next year, something that he would have plenty of time to think about.

He suddenly realized there was no time left. It was happening right now. At this very minute they were probably classifying him 1-A, putting him through the mill by paper. He made a decision. He did not want to go into the Army and he did not want to fight in Vietnam. He would apply for conscientious objector status.

The next day he went down to his draft board and asked for the CO forms. The draft secretary, however, did not even bother to get them out. She gave him a cup of coffee instead and explained in detail how very few CO exemptions were being granted and then only to Quakers or people who could prove lifetime affiliation with a church which forbade its members to kill even in wartime. John did not have a chance.

"Let me give you a piece of advice," she said. "Don't even apply. It will look bad on your record."

John went home in a cloud of gloom. Two weeks later he was drafted.

3

The Army Builds Men

On August 23, 1967, John Picciano arrived for basic training at Fort Dix, New Jersey, feeling strangely buoyant. He had dreaded going into the Army, but gradually that dread had turned to resignation and then to a kind of grudging curiosity. Fort Dix was a bustling complex of old barracks, newer brick buildings, sandy target areas, clattering mess halls, and company after company of poker-faced young men training for duty. At the entrance gates, there was a sign declaring that the Army was "an equal opportunity employer." That was more than John could say about his previous experience on the job market. Since he had not been able to get anywhere outside the Army, maybe things would change now that he was inside.

Perhaps he wouldn't be sent to Vietnam, after all. Maybe he would end up in Guam like the tanned grinning soldiers in the "see the world with the Army" posters. He mused about the possibilities. A couple of his friends had been sent to Germany; one of them had mailed home a picture of himself in a beer hall with his arms around two gorgeous blondes. He could probably learn a skill in the Army and there was always the option of going to college on a GI bill afterward. The military might not be a piece of cake, but if nothing else, it had gotten him out of the drab dead-end streets of Lodi. He wasn't a hippie or a longhair and he didn't *hate* America. He was just an ordinary guy, and in spite of all the bad things he'd read and heard about the war, the tales of brutality and senseless killing, he could keep an open mind about it if there was another side to hear. After all, he thought, he had to make the best of a bad job.

The newly arrived trainees were herded into the reception center by a husky sergeant, who sat looking them over for several minutes while massaging his knuckles, which resembled ball bearings. He asked the single men and then the married ones to raise their hands.

"Not that it makes any difference." He snickered. "I guess you guys have a problem. Everyone knows your wives are going to be fucking while you're gone."

The single men laughed and the married ones looked uncomfortable.

The next two weeks were to be the most compressed and accelerated two weeks of John's life. After twenty years of living at a slow, lazy pace, he was thrown into a highly charged atmosphere where each day seemed like a month, where each event seemed to throw him off balance. Things happened so fast that he could hardly digest one bewildering experience before another would come in its wake.

The first few days of basic after the orientation period

went by in a rush. The uninterrupted physical exer-
tion—duty at dawn, exercises, marching, exercises, more
marching—was enough to put John's body, unused to such
efforts, into a state of semishock and temporarily suspend
his thought processes. He raced from activity to activity,
bleary-eyed and exhausted. Physical training was the
worst. The drill sergeant, a dwarfed red-faced lifer from
Kentucky, would mount a platform, thrust out his bony
chest like a chicken, and call out the drill in a kind of
high-pitched scream as though the words were caught in
the back of his throat.

"Think of your life as one long push-up," he yelled to
the men lying at his feet, breathing dirt.

He liked to pick on the overweight trainees. "Get your
ass off the ground, fatso!"

If a guy was too slow, he'd order the corporal to step on
his hand.

The Army seemed to have its own peculiar laws of
logic. Halfway through the first long march, the sergeant
said it looked like rain and ordered the company to trot a
mile back to the barracks to get raincoats. When they got
back, he declared with a grin that it didn't look like rain
after all; the slickers had to be returned. Three panting
privates made the round trip a third time because they had
forgotten the elastic bands for their helmet covers. When
one of them later dropped in the line from exhaustion, the
men were ordered to walk over him until he dragged
himself up out of desperation.

By the end of the first three days John felt like a zombie.
Batting around from place to place, jerking down some
kind of a processing chute with no idea of how he would
come out in the end. He seemed to have lost a sense of his
own presence, to have left the essential John Picciano,

whatever that was, back at the reception center along with his civilian clothes, his penknife, his head of thick wavy hair. This new thing he had suddenly become —US51980146, a slightly paunchy, slightly slow-moving, slightly confused private in Company E 4/3, Fort Dix, United States Army—hardly seemed there at all. Time was losing a grip on him. The days had no beginnings, the night no end; nothing followed. Everything happened in bangs. Bang. Bellow of a sergeant blows you out of bed. Bang. Spit-shine shoes till the leather looks like a fun-house mirror. Bang. Fifty push-ups. Bang. Run two miles till you drop. Bang. Awake at 1 A.M. to flashlights shining in your face so they can see if you're asleep. Sometimes on the long marches, weariness would make his mind go blank and he would forget what he was doing. Bang. I am John Picciano. I am walking around in my own body, putting one foot in front of the other and it's called marching.

He would not have minded the physical punishment of training so much if he thought it would benefit him in the long run. He wasn't a mama's boy; he could get along. The shoving and poking, the breaking down and stripping away would have been endurable if he had got even the slightest hint that a healthy purpose lay behind it all. As it happened, any last-minute illusions he had about the military's helping him amount to something in the world were quickly shattered.

The fact that the Army had rather low expectations of its recruits was drummed into them daily by their superiors ("On your feet, dumb meat," "Get in line, you shithead"). If anyone fancied he could rise to a slightly higher level during his two-year stretch, there was a standard marching song to convince him otherwise:

I am a knucklehead, dumb dumb knucklehead
Marching down the avenue
Eight more weeks and we'll be through

The men sang the verse over and over on the short marches . . . the long marches .,. . jogging to the latrine . . . filing into the mess hall. Soon they began to believe it. The politeness, comradeliness and good manners of the first arrival days gave way to piggishness. Food riots in the mess hall were common and could be started by a simple "Pass the peas"; goodies from home had to be hidden as soon as they were received. And in nearby Wrightstown, the privates from the base, who were famous for getting falling-down drunk, were considered the lowest form of creature. Girls shunned their advances and all but the roughest and fastest townies considered themselves hard up if they had to go out with a soldier.

The majority of trainees were not deeply affected by the peculiarly humiliating position in which military life put them. The handful of upper-middle-class men who had managed to get drafted found it easy to treat basic as a joke. Better educated and less intimidated by authority figures, they knew how to avoid getting picked on by the sergeants and they also knew that it would all end well; they would be able to wangle their way into good, comfortable as-signments far from the front lines of Vietnam. As for the rest, sons of farmers and factory workers, their sanity seemed to be preserved by their ability to conform. They could sing the "knucklehead song" gustily and without embarrassment. They could take abuse from the sergeants and give it back to each other without much inner turmoil, for they were all in it together. It was as though somewhere they thought that as long as they were *all* functioning as animals, they weren't *really* animals at all. It was only the nonconformists, the very bright or very dumb, the too fat or the too thin, the introverts and loners who had trouble playing the game.

The game included passing a quart of White Horse around the barracks late on the odd night. John relished the moments alone in bed when he could lie back and let his pent-up mind repair itself. He dreaded hearing the padding of feet after lights out, the rattle of a paper bag, and the muffled laughs and whispers which meant that the night was just beginning. He frankly did not like to drink. But the military seemed to change everyone; no one was allowed to be his own man even when the sergeants weren't around.

"Hey, we've got a bottle here. Have a drink," one of the guys would say.

"No, thanks, I don't drink much."

"You better drink. What's the matter with you, anyway?"

In the end, John took the drink.

The Army had a sophisticated technique for bringing out the best in its trainees on the battlefield. Anxiety was created, as if by design, as early as 5 A.M., when the lights flooded on, bunks were kicked, and men were expected to awake and dress in the same sixty-second interval. Then came inspection, waiting rumpled and rankled in line, each wondering whether this was the day he would be singled out as the slob. By the time bayonet practice rolled around most were so angry they speared their stuffed targets with the bloodlust of samurais. Neck muscles straining, they would run forward yelling, "Kill, kill, kill," each time their left feet touched the ground, looking spent and fulfilled after they had made their hits.

John had a very different reaction. He felt only embarrassed and flustered as he pretended to mouth the battle cries and tried in vain to feel something personal toward the dummy he was about to slay. At first, bayonet and rifle practice had not been entirely unpleasant. Pumping bullets into cardboard figures was, in fact, a kind of fun break from the rest of the grinding routine. Then, one day a sergeant gave a lecture extolling the virtues of the M-14 rifle. It was, the sergeant said, a fabulous gun; it could send a bullet through a tree and kill a man standing on the other side.

The remark had brought John up short, and the reality of what he was doing, where he was going, flashed through his mind. Kill. Killing. The words took life, were no longer random shouts, obscenities, football cheers. They meant pain, suffering, the mutilation not of cardboard but of flesh and blood. The horror stories recited by his Vietnam veteran friends at home, which seemed so fantastic then, were very real to him now. Something was happening here, day in and day out, as he panted through the two-mile runs, learned to crawl on his belly and shoot from his hip. It was not only that the Army was chipping away at his ego, bringing him down to grunt size so he would obey without question for the duration of his service. It was what they were trying to make him into that frightened him. A perfectly regular guy could come into the Army, and before he knew it, he was doing things he'd never done before. Making fun of some poor fat guy after the sergeants had kicked him around. Talking about what it would be like to get a gang together and take the bus-terminal café waitress out in the alley. If you were bullied long enough, all the base and mean-spirited instincts pushed themselves to the surface and they would be honed sharp as the edges of swords. You didn't think twice about shoving a bayonet into the belly of a straw dummy, and when the time came, you probably wouldn't think too much about shoving it into the belly of a man.

He began to have trouble sleeping. He could perform during the day without giving himself away. When others fell down on the marches, he always made it through to the end and he deliberately avoided asking questions. The sergeants didn't pay much attention to him and none of them suspected how much trouble he was having inside. It all came out at night. The television newsreels he had seen of the war began to obsess him; marines putting their Zippos to the "hooches" in South Vietnamese villages; the twisted, agonized faces of the refugees; rows of body bags waiting to be carried off in helicopters; 2,000 American casualties a week. He had a recurring nightmare. He was sitting at a desk in the Lodi Public Library and all of a sudden the light bulbs started popping and he was in a field. Guns were going off and the sky was red and children were running around yelling, "Kill, kill," and hurling tall stalks of grass which turned into knives as soon as they left their hands. He would awake shaking, his pajamas soaked with sweat. His bunkmate below hurled pillows at him, cursing at the creaking of the bed. The infirmary duty nurses said the problem was indigestion and prescribed two aspirins before retiring.

There seemed to be only one choice left for him. The thought of it would have terrified him before he had gone into the Army. It had never occurred to him then to defy his induction notice or to put up any kind of resistance to the U.S. Army. He had been in the service for only two weeks, not long enough really to give it a try, but he knew he had to do something and fast. He was getting sicker and sicker, spending sleepless nights, eating so little he was weak most of the time. He wondered whether all this was worth going through for a war that a lot of people were against and nobody else seemed to give a damn about. Things were nearing a climax for him, and there seemed to be only one way out. He decided to go AWOL.

When he arrived in Lodi, his parents were out, so he left a note telling them he was going up to Canada to talk with a group he had heard about—the Toronto Anti-Draft Programme. The draft resistance movement had been gaining momentum throughout the fall; draft resistance unions were cropping up all over the country and rallies had whipped up massive support in even the small towns for a national Stop the Draft Week beginning October 16. Although the movement was aimed at the student or middle-class boy facing induction rather than those who had already been conscripted into service, the winds of change had begun to filter into the bases. John had read about the case of Captain Howard Levy, who that spring had refused to train Green Beret medical aid men on the grounds they were "killers of peasants and children" and had been sent to prison for his stand. Antiwar protesters had leafletted Fort Dix several times and he had got the name of the Toronto outfit from one of them.

John was getting a little nervous as he walked up Spadina Avenue in Toronto toward the building where the antidraft group was located. Absent Without Leave. Illegal. Did he want that? What was he doing anyway? He had never broken the law in his life. Always on the straight and narrow. Even in high school when the guys were stealing hubcaps, his daredevil would leave him and he'd stay on the sidelines, watching. He'd defaced a toilet wall at Pap's Luncheonette once. Written some graffiti underneath the sink. But that was about all. He didn't know whether he really wanted to go over the hill. It would mean a lot of trouble. More trouble than if he stayed in, maybe. In any case, this was only an AWOL. Not so bad, really. Guys did it all the time. He knew of three who had gone AWOL and nothing too bad had happened to them. He had had to get out of that place for a while, at least, even if it meant going into the stockade for a week. He had to get out and think about the whole thing.

It was good to be far from Fort Dix, to be walking up this avenue in Toronto. The air was clear; normal people were doing normal things; there were greengrocers with Italian names on the awnings; pots and pails piled up on the sidewalk in front of hardware stores. A man was soliciting customers outside a burlesque theater.

Inside the antidraft office longhairs and women in miniskirts milled around. It was a small, dingy room full of overstuffed chairs and old Remingtons. He would probably have to wait a long time. There was a pile of unsorted mail on one desk. He was glancing idly at it when his eyes fell on a Western Union envelope which carried his name. His heart leaped. He ripped open the telegram. It was from his parents: COME HOME. MOTHER ILL.

So much for deserting, he thought. He caught the first bus back. It was a good thing he had got a round-trip ticket—he had bought it only because he had heard that if you were caught AWOL, they couldn't charge you with desertion as long as you had a return ticket in your pocket.

He had been in Canada only six hours and it was as if he hadn't been there at all.

At home on River Street, Constance Picciano was distraught. She had been seized with stomach cramps and chills as soon as she read the note from her son. John Picciano, Sr., had called the relatives, who hurried over from the Bronx to comfort Constance and take a hand in sending the wire. They were all waiting together when John returned home. His aunts were bustling and twittering around, tidying up the already clean kitchen and brewing coffee. The tiny living room sounded like an aviary. He was glad to be back in familiar surroundings, back to his home, in spite of the uproar that was going on inside it. The house looked just the same but a little strange, smaller, as though he had gone away as a child and come back full-grown. It seemed as if he had been away a lot longer than two weeks. It was good to see the table he had made standing just where he left it and the bookcases, filled with his encyclopedia and some new volumes of *Reader's Digest* that he hadn't seen before.

Constance embraced him, weeping. "What are you trying to do to me, Johnny? It's not like you to run away like that. You can't do this. I'll get sick."

John calmed his mother until she had collected herself enough to fix a ravioli dinner for all the aunts and uncles and cousins, and they spent the evening trying to talk him out of deserting the Army.

"Look, son," said his father. "It won't be good if you leave. Just do this one thing, even if you don't want to, and it'll be over soon. It's bad, OK, but you just gotta take it. You been called, what are you gonna do? Nothing you can do. You just gotta take it."

John knew he had to relent, if only for the sake of his mother. He told his father he would go back. He'd try to make a go of it again. Maybe he'd get used to it. Maybe it would just go away. The Piccianos drove him back to Fort Dix the next morning, having got him to promise he'd stay put and, if he didn't, to let them know before he did anything rash.

Once again, he was deposited into the chaos, the mad frantic machine which was playing tricks on his mind. He would try to beat it, to stick it out as his father had begged him to do, but he had his doubts as to how it would all end.

John was not put in the stockade, as he had expected. He soon found out, however, that his AWOL had cost him something else. They knew him now. The sergeants looked at him a little differently, watched him a little more closely. He had blown his carefully nurtured anonymity, and he found himself cleaning latrines twice a day. One black sergeant with dark glasses kept eyeing him with what could only be described as pure hate. The sergeant, his corporal in tow, stopped him one day in front of the mess hall and gave him a long look up and down.

"Hey, boy, what you got there?" He lifted up John's chin. "What you got on your chin?"

He turned to his corporal. "He needs a shave, he's a pig, man. He's a real pig."

"Go get a shave, Picciano." He slapped John's cheeks lightly and walked away.

The base seemed kind of remote now that he had been out in the real world. Everything looked far away and he felt isolated, somehow detached from the helter-skelter movements that went on around him, as if he were slightly deaf or myopic. Time stretched out interminably and the first twenty-four hours he was back seemed like a week.

On the marches, he would think that they had been going for at least half an hour and look down at his watch to find that only five minutes had gone by. The potatoes were worse; cleaning them up after they had been through the peeling machine seemed impossible, as though he were in some surreal fantasy where the eyes grew back as soon as he had cut them out.

He would nod off during the movies. The Army had an unending series of them—on the destructive power of the Cobra gunship, on communist propaganda ("They have ways of making you believe lies about your government and Wall Street"), on communist prison camps ("Worse than anything you've ever heard about"). There was one on the Military Code of Conduct featuring a "real-life situation" in which a mean little Oriental with a Bugs Bunny smile interrogated big strapping American soldiers. The Americans, their faces pressed into grimly determined expressions, were led into a bare room and shoved under spotlights, just like in the FBI TV show. They all remained firm under severe interrogation, repeating over and over name, rank, and serial number, except for a thin effeminate GI who finally broke into tears and spilled the beans about the location of his buddies. "The one who broke," remarked the instructor, "is the type of guy the Army doesn't want."

John kept meeting Vietnam veterans. They seemed to be everywhere. There were a lot of them on the base, enlisted men who had come back as NCO's with medals and promotions, and they didn't talk about the war. They stiffened when you brought it up, and if you asked what was going on over there, what it was all about, they never gave you a straight answer. Many of them were intense, nervous men who walked quickly and talked fast. He had heard friends of his father go on and on about their exploits in World War II, recounting tales of heroism and courage, stories of Nazi terror brought to an end because of the daring exploits of Allied soldiers, incidents which were smattered with suspense, humor, pathos. The Vietnam veterans at Fort Dix told no such war stories. They did not speak well of the war, nor did they speak badly of it, as some of the young veterans in Lodi had. If they did mention Vietnam, it was in general terms. "Charlie's tough, private, so you better learn your bayonet now because you won't have a chance to relearn it over there. If you don't kill him, he'll kill you."

Basic training was beginning to take its toll of many of the trainees. The specter of Vietnam loomed ever larger and the privates sang dark, sardonic ditties: "Be the first one on your block/ to be brought home in a box." AWOL's were frequent, as were cases of insubordination, and minor acts of rebellion were punished by time in the stockade. There was a lot of talk about ways to get out of training and into a clerk's job or out of the Army altogether. There were those who took extreme measures—one recruit sat down in the middle of calisthenics and began rocking and singing lullabies; another blew his toe off on the rifle range. An epileptic who was inducted because the Army doctors refused to believe he wasn't lying about his condition in order to avoid the draft was finally discharged after several convincing fits. One eighteen-year-old went to more extreme measures. Obese, slow, and sloppy, he was the target of mockery by his peers and abuse by his sergeants, who would beat and kick him because he could do no more than five push-ups and constantly dropped on marches. One day he was found in the latrine, hanging by his neck.

When John heard about it, he thought he understood

why the boy had done it. He knew, however, that there was a better way to get out of the Army. He walked off the base and headed for Lodi.

His parents once again tried to persuade him to go back, his mother pleading that she would become ill, his father arguing that it had only been a few days since his last AWOL and he should give it a longer time, his aunts and cousins coming over from the Bronx. For the sake of peace, he agreed to return, knowing inside that what they were asking him to do was probably, in the long run, impossible. It had taken only a few weeks; but the Army had eaten away at him like an ulcer, and now the pain was no longer dull, nor would it subside. He could not go back, not now, and maybe not ever. The family took him down to the station and put him on a bus for Wrightstown, smiling relieved smiles, thinking that he would go back once and for all to do what he had to do. At the first stop outside Lodi, John got off and caught another bus bound for Toronto.

This time his actions were more determined. He had bought only a one-way ticket and he had withdrawn his small savings of about $200 from his bank in Lodi. It wouldn't go far, he knew, but at least he would have enough to get by on until he decided what to do, exactly which way to turn. As before, he had a surprisingly easy time crossing the border. The immigration men passed him through quickly as a visitor. His short, obviously military haircut did not raise suspicions.

He felt nervous, more nervous than before, as he entered the Toronto Anti-Draft Programme office. He could feel his feet sweating. The office wasn't so crowded this time. He almost wished it were. He didn't want to go up to anybody, so he just sat down on a torn-up sofa, on the spot where the stuffing was coming out. There were posters and literature all over the room on draft dodging. But he didn't belong in that category. He was a deserter. Someone who could be shot during wartime. Perhaps he was the first deserter to walk through these doors.

A tall guy with a bush of curly blond hair was watching him. His feet were sweating so much his socks were soaked. They probably smelled terrible. Maybe the guy could smell them all the way over where he was sitting behind an old wooden desk.

"Can I help you?" the draft counselor said, and got up and came over.

"Ahhh—yes. Well, I just came up from New Jersey." This was it. He was actually doing it. Talking to a subversive. Asking for help to break the law. Three more people came in. "Um, could we go somewhere a little more private?"

The two walked out of the office, through a door leading to a fire escape and then down to an alley in back of the building. They sat on the steps. The guy looked friendly and easygoing, and that helped John say the words he'd dreaded saying.

"I'm a deserter." He had lost the end of the word in a slur. It sounded as if he were saying he was something you had after the main dinner course. He waited for the shock to register on the guy's face, for him to recoil a bit. But his face didn't change. "I'm not a draft dodger," John tried again. "I left the Army."

"So what?" The guy smiled and shrugged. "Look, take it easy, man. It's OK. We hear a lot of guys are doing it now. A lot of them are beginning to desert the Army."

"Yeah?" Relief eased John's body. Perhaps this wasn't

so bad after all. Nobody was going to throw rocks at him. Maybe he had a lot of company. "Look, do you think if this was a different war, a different army, say like in World War II, that people would be doing this, dodging the draft and deserting? I mean, do you think I . . . someone like me, would be doing this if it was a different kind of war?"

"No, I don't think they would be," the counselor answered.

They returned to the office and John met others who worked on the "programme," as the Canadians spelled it. It was run by Canadian students and activists along with American draft resisters. They looked at him with admiration and shook his hand. Almost 500 draft evaders had crossed the border and been granted permission to live in Canada since the resistance movement got under way in the spring, they explained. To everyone's surprise, they had been received well in the press and Canadians treated them with respect. John was one of the first GI's who had appeared, they said, but the antiwar groups were making a big push to organize inside the bases and they expected a lot more deserters might follow.

The blond counselor phoned the Canadian Immigration Department, where draft dodgers went as a matter of course to get "landed"—receive immigrant status—and made an appointment for John the following afternoon. "Don't worry, there won't be any problem," he said. "We'll fix you up here, get you some papers and find you a place to live. It's going to be OK, man. There's a lot of people here who will help you."

At the immigration office, John filled out an application to become a landed immigrant to Canada and then waited an hour to meet the interviewing officer. The atmosphere was impersonal and utilitarian in comparison to the warmth of the antidraft place, and the officer was brisk. He seemed surprised when John told him he had left the Army and wanted to live and work in Canada. He would have to wait for a while, the officer said, while he had the application okayed by his superiors.

John sat back and looked around. He hoped the look the officer had given him didn't mean that there would be any trouble. No, the antidraft counselor had assured him that his application would be accepted. Perhaps he was just imagining the officer's look. Yes, he probably was. Draft dodgers walked into the immigration office every day. The officers must be used to antiwar Americans by now. He had to get over his paranoia about what he was doing. It really didn't seem so terrible now that he was out of the Army. People outside looked at the whole thing differently. Going AWOL these days no longer meant going berserk, crazy, out of your mind, and out of the world. After all, draft dodgers had respectability. A lot of big shots, clergymen, writers, politicians were urging them to defy the Army. What was the difference then between going into the Army for a few weeks before getting out and not going in at all? He was just as good as any draft dodger. If he had known how to do it, how to burn his draft card, if he had known where to go to learn what to do or if anybody had been around to stand behind him while he did it, he never would have answered his induction notice. He thought the people at the Anti-Draft Programme realized that. They didn't consider him strange. They looked up to him and that was a good feeling. Yes, he felt good about it. At least, he had *done* something, something concrete about the hell that was around him. Having done that, having resisted, gave him a respect that being a "soldier" hadn't. Here he was kind of a hero. There he had been a piece of shit.

It was being a piece of shit that he couldn't handle. Everybody was shit, grunts, knuckleheads, in basic. But wasn't that the way in all armies? Hadn't the last generation gone through the same indignities in training in order to get the steel to defeat the highly trained Nazis and the kamikaze Japanese? Maybe it was just his own weakness. Maybe he just couldn't take it. He'd always been a bookish, private person. Never went out for football or feats of physical daring. Shying away whenever possible from strenuous exercises. Perhaps that was his downfall. Maybe he just didn't have what it took to be, well, what the Army called a real "man." Someone who had a dick like a 155mm cannon and a right hook which flashed forth at the first sign of danger or insult, who fathered five children and kept two or three mistresses happy on the side, who made twenty-five grand a year, and filled his bookcases with war medals and bowling trophies. Perhaps he was just an all-time loser. Would he have fought in World War II? Would he have happily dug into the trenches, gritted his teeth, and sprayed down as many Nips as he could lay eyes on? At least then he would have known why he had to do it. Pearl Harbor might have produced a hate great enough for him to slice throats and pump bullets into human beings without hesitation, without remorse. He would have been doing it for his mother and father, for the wife and kids back home, for his own physical freedom. Yes, he was sure he could have done it then; he could have killed someone who had helped invade his own country or someone who participated in sending a whole race to the gas chambers. But how could he hate a Vietcong enough to kill him? How could he ever learn to despise someone ten thousand miles away and come to believe that that person was threatening him, had to be eliminated if he was to survive? It was all so turned around, this war. Who did you believe anyway? Should he take on faith the argument that it was necessary for the freedom of his country, for his own personal freedom in the long run, that he fight this war, maybe die for it. How could he *really* know? He had never been to Vietnam, and the Vietnamese had never been here.

Perhaps he had to follow his instincts. Maybe when you didn't know all the answers, you had to rely on your *sense* of a thing to tell you what to do. Back at Fort Dix, he had had a bad feeling almost constantly, like perpetual indigestion. Every morning when he woke up, something was telling him, "You shouldn't be here. This is not right," and it wasn't just a rebellion against the rough treatment or the fact that every minute of his life belonged to the Army. It was another kind of feeling, the kind you get at a party when you keep taking another drink to be sociable long after you don't want any more. There was something he was fighting against in the Army, some kind of intrusion. During bayonet practice this internal battle would rage strong, as though all his white blood cells were marshaling to repel some invading virus. It left him weak, confused, and miserable.

When he was very small, he had played with a toy rifle, running and hiding in the bushes, felling imaginary enemies. He used to love Westerns and the John Wayne war movies which made heroes out of cowards and real men out of shambling nobodies. Once he thought how much fun it would be to become a general and plan attacks and move flags on pins around a papier-mâché battlefield. He never guessed what it would be like to be grown up and wriggling underneath one of those pins.

Now that he was underneath, it would be hard to get out, harder than he dared imagine. Leaving everything he knew, just walking out on nineteen years of his past. Did he dare do it? All his life he had been taught to stay in line. If he just did what he was told, if he rode with the punches, he would be all right, they said. But if he strayed, God help him.

What would he do? Where would he go, with $200, a military ID card, and one black suit with worn knees? How could he get a job in some foreign country with a high school diploma and no skills? There would be whispers on River Street. His parents would be broken up. How's your son, Connie? What's he doing now? they would ask his mother months from now and she would probably burst into tears and turn the other way, unable even to lie about it. His father would most likely be snubbed at the factory. His son is a pinko, they would say. And he would be running, always running, maybe never ever able to return to his country, to his home, to Lodi, which he had never been away from for more than two weeks at a time. The thought of that made him shiver. His feet broke out into a second sweat.

There was no sign of the immigration officer. What was taking so long? He had already waited more than two hours. Waiting, all this waiting. He felt like he had been waiting all his life, waiting for something to happen. Maybe it was happening now.

As long as he could remember, he had been on the fringes, slightly set apart from his school, his teachers, his friends. In some ways, he had been satisfied with that; he had liked living on his own terms. Being outside, however, had been painful and lonely. He had always hoped that someday he would find a place in the world where he could do something, be somebody, where there would be people who understood and could talk to him. Now, here he was, further isolating himself, this time not just mentally, but *physically*. He was pulling up anchor and setting out for nowhere, perhaps to drift on and on into anonymity. Was this his destiny? Was leaving the Army just another step in the logical progression of his life thus far?

He remembered one time when he was seven or eight years old playing kickball on the school playground. Each time it was his turn to kick, he missed. He just couldn't seem to connect his foot with the ball. Everyone was making fun of him, calling him names, and he wanted more than anything to just run off, to tell them he didn't have to take this and could find better things to do. But he didn't dare. It was easier to stay and take it than to walk away from it and be called a scaredy-cat, easier to play their game instead of his, easier to endure the pain than to get rid of it.

Pain. The whole concept of pain could have you in circles if you thought too much about it. Was he letting himself in for worse pain now by trying to ease the old one? Just imagining what would happen to him if he left the Army was a kind of mental pain in itself. So now he had two sources of pain. But clearly the first pain was worse. Like if somebody pinches you on one arm and then pinches you on the other, the second pinch doesn't matter so much, you are just concerned with getting rid of the first. What if he got caught, apprehended by the FBI? Then he would have two *real* pains. But if you had so much pain to begin with, would a little more matter?

He'd better stop thinking. He was getting more and more confused. He could probably sit and think the whole thing into the ground until he had grown a white beard and was stuck to the chair. There came a time when you just had to stop trying to figure out what was the right choice to make, forget about everything else and just decide one-two-three. Every choice had its consequences and there came a time when you just had to take a gamble that the consequences wouldn't be too bad. He had made a choice and he was glad of it. Yes, all in all, he felt good about it. Perhaps it takes a kind of courage to walk away.

"Mr. Picciano? Mr. Picciano!" The interviewing officer had come back into the room. He looked apprehensive and worried. "Mr. Picciano, I'm afraid your application has not been accepted."

"What?"

"We cannot grant you permission to live here. The application was checked out very thoroughly and I'm afraid it's out of the question."

It knocked the wind out of him. The officer was talking and he couldn't even hear him. The room was swaying.

". . . I'm very much afraid that we must take you into custody for deportation."

Two Royal Canadian Mounted Police, their heavy boots clacking on the parquet floor, entered the room, lifted him up from his chair, and marched him toward the door.

"Wait, wait, will you wait a minute!" John struggled, tried to yank his arms free. He could feel their holstered guns bumping against his hip.

The RCMP's tightened their grip. "Come along quietly, son, or it will be worse for you."

"Oh, look, this is ridiculous, this is stupid!" He tried to grab onto something. "You're making a mistake. You don't pick up draft dodgers!"

"You're not a draft dodger. You're a deserter. Come along now."

John was hardly aware of where he was being taken, everything happened so fast after that. The squad car whipped through the streets of Toronto. He was led into a building, down some long corridors, and into a room. A door was locked behind him and he suddenly found himself in jail, along with a handful of drunks and derelicts. The cell stank. One old man who wore several layers of rumpled clothes slept slumped in the corner; two others with unshaven beards were muttering to themselves. One of them kept patting the empty seat beside him and motioning to John, but he smelled so bad that John remained standing.

Finally the name Picciano was called and a guard took him into another room, where he was told to strip to his shorts. His personal belongings and his wallet were thoroughly looked over and then locked in a file drawer. Another guard presided while he took a shower, was sprayed with disinfectant and fitted out in gray prison clothes.

He ended up in a small cagelike room in a larger cell block. The room was about 8 by 10 feet with two narrow cots on either wall and just enough room to stand up between them. They brought him food and it tasted like paste, the toilets at the end of the cell block were open only from 7 A.M. to 7 P.M., and John just lay on his cot trying to think about nothing.

The next day his name was erased from a long list on a blackboard at the end of the cell block. He was given his civilian clothes, escorted to the airport, and put on a plane bound for Buffalo. He slept through the flight, shutting his mind off from all thought of what was happening to him.

After landing, two armed policemen boarded the plane and took John down the gangplank while the rest of the passengers remained seated. They grabbed him tightly by the upper arms and quickstepped him through the airport so fast his feet were half skimming the ground. One of them remarked to the other that he thought John's skin looked a little yellow. An old lady came up to them as they were waiting for a squad car and stared at John with wide eyes for several minutes. He gave her a goblin face and she fled.

At the city jail, his belt was taken away and he was put into another cell. He laid down on a cot and tried to think about the banks of the Saddle River.

"Hey, don't make yourself comfortable, buddy," said one of the policemen. "You have company."

Two military police strode in and dragged John to his feet. "This guy been frisked yet?"

"Nope, we left that for you."

Outside the jailhouse, the MP's pushed him up against the wall, kicked his legs out, and whacked his arms up with a truncheon. They handcuffed his wrists behind his back and shoved him into a car so hard that his head hit the door and his glasses fell off and were smashed underneath his feet.

"Sorry about that, soldier," said the MP who took the driver's seat. "Don't matter anyhow since they belonged to the Army just like your ass." The military green Chevrolet Biscayne took off with a roar toward Niagara Falls Air Force Base.

"What are we doing, the Indianapolis Five Hundred?" said John.

"Shut your mouth, meathead."

John was put into the stockade at Niagara Falls for a couple of days until enough other Fort Dix AWOL's had been brought in to fill up a bus to go to Wrightstown.

One of the Niagara AFB prisoners was a drug addict and he had sat for twenty-four hours in agony. They had put him in a cell by himself; his mouth foamed at the corners and he was banging his head on the bars. Finally,

the guards came and tied him onto a stretcher and took him
away in an ambulance.

"Anyone for some smack," cracked one inmate as he
was wheeled out of the stockade.

The bus trip was long and hot, only one window would
open, and the MP's walked up and down the aisles
periodically like guards watching their prisoners. No one
talked; everyone knew how much trouble he was in.

John watched the wide rolling spaces of upper New
York State go by and a sad hollow feeling overtook him.
They passed farms and pastures where cattle were grazing
lazily and ponies wandered loose. Picnickers sat underneath the trees which were beginning to turn yellow, red,
gold. So much for deserting. Nothing ever seemed to
change for him. There must be a force greater than himself
that decided his fate, that worked like a magnet to pull him
back into line whenever he ventured out. If so, he was
powerless. Nothing he could do. Perhaps in the end, he
was never meant to be free. The air in the bus was stale and
gaseous. He would steel himself for whatever came. No
more thinking now. He needed to numb his body and
mind so he would be only half-conscious to receive the
punishments they had in store for him.

When they arrived at Fort Dix, the busload of
AWOL's were conducted into the provost marshal's office
to wait for several hours until they had been reprocessed.
"If you make one peep," said an MP, "I'll lock you all in
and you can shit yourselves to death."

John was put into solitary confinement for twenty-four
hours and then into the regular stockade along with an
assorted group of military misfits—drug offenders,
AWOL's, men charged with theft, rape, homosexual acts.
There were several who acted crazy, because they either

were crazy or were just trying to get out of the Army. One of them lunged at John and tried to pull his hair out, and he was later given a discharge. A homosexual who made advances to one of the men in front of a guard wasn't so lucky. His wrists and ankles were bound together with a long leather strap for four hours.

Evenings were the worst. People just sat around. There was nothing to do, no cards, no books, no TV. The only pleasure allowed was smoking and everyone, even non-smokers, acquired cigarettes because they could be used to bribe extra food or for protection money so the guards wouldn't lay into you so hard. Out of boredom, John took up smoking.

Stockade work, as well as stockade treatment, made basic look like a summer camp. Certain jobs around the base, picking up cigarette butts, or cartridge shells on the rifle range, were reserved for stockade inmates, and if there was no work to be done, they would march in circles around the yard or hold their duffel bags high above their heads for thirty minutes. If someone dropped the bag before the time was up, he would receive a club in the chest.

They lived on what the men called rabbit chow—lettuce, bread, potatoes, beans—and drank their water out of bowls. There were no dairy products or meat of any kind save for the occasional worm which was found in the lettuce. Those who had been there more than a week were pale and suffering from weight loss.

One day John and several others were given what they considered a break: washing cars belonging to the brass and weeding crabgrass from the lawns. It was a sunny day and the men were feeling frisky from being relieved of the usual backbreaking duties. Two of the inmates who were

spraying down a general's car became engaged in a small
water fight and a guard, who had a flat face and an upper lip
which exposed his gums, came up and shoved them both
against the car.

"You fuckin' walrus," one of the men exploded.

The guard grabbed and grounded him, training the hose
into his mouth until water was running out of his nose and
he was gasping for breath.

"Hey, what the hell are you doing?" yelled John, who
was pulling up grass nearby.

The guard abandoned the choking inmate and turned
on John. "You ain't pulling that grass very fast, troop," he
said and brought his bat down hard on John's hand, splin-
tering the bone in his left middle finger.

John knew it was broken and asked to see a doctor to get
the break set, but the guard who was responsible encouraged him to let it heal naturally.

"You don't need a doctor yet, Picciano, but you *will*
need one if you mention this to anybody."

John went from the stockade straight into the Special
Processing Detachment, a small company of men who had
shown no signs of assimilating into Army life and who
were therefore given massive doses of it. A typical day
began at 3:15 A.M., when the SPD men would rise and
begin a daylong process of feeding and cleaning up after
trainees out on field operations. They loaded food, bivouac
supplies, and garbage pails full of water onto a truck, drove
it out to the field site, served the food, cleaned up, and
brought the empty pots and pails back, sterilized them, and
began all over again for lunch and then again for dinner.
They were finished about 8 P.M. in time to get in two
hours of exercises and training before bed at 10:30.

After two days of it, John was exhausted and edgy. The SPD men were confined to a small area, and even when they went to the mess hall, they were accompanied by a military policeman. At lunch he met Sammy White, a friend from Lodi who had enlisted in July.

"Hey, John, you look bad," said Sammy.

"Haven't had more than four hours' sleep the last two nights."

"I heard about your AWOL's. What's happening anyway?"

"I just don't like the Army, that's all." He could never have explained why to Sammy White, who was not like John at all.

"I don't like it either, but you can't let it get to you. You gotta laugh at it."

John held up his misshapen finger. "You gonna laugh at that?"

The MP tapped John on the shoulder. "Come on, it's time to get back."

Back to SPD, back to scouring the kitchen equipment. John picked up a Brillo pad lackadaisically and started cleaning soot off the pipes of an antiquated heating unit which he had just desooted that morning. Useless work. Hours wasted out of his life. No matter how much you reasoned with the Army, it wouldn't listen. He couldn't laugh at it, like Sammy White; he could only feel anger and contempt. He wished he could rub a Brillo pad in a sergeant's mug, rub it so hard the skin came clean.

"Hurry up, Picciano," said the platoon leader, a lean, slightly effeminate reservist from Boston. "It'll be dirty again before you're through."

"Oh, fuck off."

"What?"

John threw the Brillo pad down on the floor. "Fuck off."
The platoon leader pursed his lips and turned.

"Well, I can't take responsibility for this. I'll have to call
a sergeant."

John was escorted off by two corporals and delivered to
the company commanding officer, who sat behind a desk
in a large office. He looked John over.

"You're dirty, Private."

"Yes, sir." John was covered with soot and had a four
o'clock beard. "They didn't give me a chance to clean up,
sir."

"At ease!" The commanding officer was telling John to
shut up. He turned to the corporals. "Maybe we should put
a pot over his head and make him dry shave so we don't
have to look at his ugly face."

"I was cleaning the heating unit for the second time
today, sir. It just gets dirty again. It doesn't make any
sense."

"At ease! I'm sick of looking at your face. Get him out of
here. Take him to the colonel."

John was glad for the chance to see the lieutenant
colonel of his battalion. In fact, he had asked to see him
several times before, but the request had always been
refused. If he couldn't succeed in extricating himself from
the Army, at least he could confront it head on, go to the
top, and lay down his grievances once and for all. The
brass might listen to reason; certainly once they understood that a man really didn't want to be in the Army,
couldn't perform well because his desire to get out was so
strong, they wouldn't actually *want* him in . . . would
they?

"What seems to be the trouble, Picciano?" The colonel,

as befitted his higher rank, had a distinctly smoother style than that of the commanding officer, a lieutenant. He was tall, straight, and smelled of English Leather.

"Sir, I cannot sleep at night, I break out in a sweat when I pick up a rifle, and I am nauseous most of the time."

"There's nothing wrong with you. You just don't like the Army, right?"

"But it's more than that, sir. I don't think I have what it takes to be an American Fighting Man."

"Don't be smart. I know a lot of people who are saying the same thing, and when they continue to say these things, they become disciplinary problems. We have to punish them and put them in the stockade and then their parents call up, crying, and I have to tell them I cannot do anything for them. How would your mother and father feel about it if you went back to the stockade, Picciano?"

"I don't think I can adjust, sir. If you'll listen to me, I'll tell you. It's that I get sick just thinking about the war. . . ."

"Now look, Picciano, I don't want to hear any more. I'm giving you a direct order. You finish your training without any more trouble or I guarantee you'll get six months in the stockade and then a court-martial and a dishonorable discharge with at least five years in a federal prison."

"But, sir! About the war, I wouldn't be any good to the Army in Vietnam. I. . . ."

"You just do what you're told, Picciano, and you will be sent where you have to be sent. I'm giving you the rest of the day off to see the chaplain. Then you think it over. Dismissed."

John's heart sank. Being sent "where you have to be sent" meant Vietnam. It was a well-known fact that the Army punished rebels and misfits with assignments to

Nam. There was one last resort. He headed for the chapel to talk to the Army chaplain—the first time he had talked with a man of the cloth since he stopped going to mass a year earlier.

He was a short, corpulent figure with a balding head, blank eyes, and a habit of clearing his throat several times before each sentence. He seemed impatient with John's complaints.

"Don't fret so much, son. You can be godly and be a soldier too, you know."

"Can I be godly and kill?"

The chaplain opened the Bible to the Book of Joshua. "Here Joshua takes the city of Jericho. The Lord helps him defeat and destroy his enemies."

"But I have no enemy in Vietnam."

"Your enemy is the communists, for they are God's enemy also. Do you know communists in Vietnam torture priests? Communists all over the world have a history of torturing priests. They are all atheists."

"But I don't want to kill or be killed in Vietnam. Isn't that a Christian desire?"

The chaplain rose wearily. "It's late now. Go back and pray to God to make you a better soldier."

Back at the billets, there was a long line heading to the latrine. John stopped and stared.

"Better go now, Picciano, this is the last chance you'll have before bedtime, thanks to shitface here."

A red-faced private was being cuffed by two of his comrades. He had asked to be excused from an exercise to go to the latrine because he had the runs. The sergeant had responded by declaring that toilet functions would be rationed since the men obviously couldn't regulate themselves.

John passed the line in disgust and went to sit on the back steps. Organized toilet training. That was the supreme insult. They had done that in grade school. Memories of Lodi flashed into his mind. The cafeteria, French bread flying through the air, kids seeing who could burp the loudest . . . graduation, with Jerry Tamburello pounding backs straight, marching his boys through the procession like soldiers . . . gangs closing in on Sal Campanella, the neighborhood's budding fag . . . his father home from the factory talking about the same things he talked about ten years earlier . . . teachers telling you not to get any ideas, you're not so great . . . one long dull gray day after another, days without surprise, without promise. Now it was the same, only worse. The military was just an exaggeration, a caricature, of all that had gone before.

It was dark now. The sound of flushing in the latrine had stopped. He supposed they would be looking for him soon. The moon was brighter than he had ever seen it and cast a wavering surreal light on the rows of barracks. A platoon was marching in the distance. The men seemed to melt into each other so you couldn't tell where one ended and the next began. He had a vision of having been born on a train full of nobodies, which just kept going, chugging past station after station, never stopping, bound for nowhere.

A feeling of suffocation came over him. He had got into something he could never get out of. That train *was* going to stop. It was all going to end, it was ending now—but not in the beer halls of Frankfurt or on the beaches of Guam. The reality of it came crashing down. He saw it clearly as if it were before him: his person, still, white, and rigid, emptied of all dreams and agonies, enclosed, nailed shut, and lowered onto a stack of long wooden boxes.

He didn't stop to collect his belongings or turn to see if

he was being watched. He just began walking, briskly, through the encampment, across the McGuire Air Force field, over roads and vacant lots, into Wrightstown.

As he approached the bus terminal, two NCO's reeled out of a bar and, noticing that he had on green fatigues instead of the required off-base dress uniform, grabbed him by the sleeve.

"Whaddya doing, going over the hill?"

"Yup," said John, who knew they wouldn't dare take him in and risk charges of drunkenness. "You planning to do something about it?"

The pair staggered off.

By the time he reached Lodi it was past midnight. He took apart the lock on the back door, crept up to his room, and packed a bag full of books and clothes. He changed into his only suit, the $60 black wool affair which had seen him confirmed and graduated and had been made over several times, and threw his fatigues on the bed. He crept out again without waking his parents. This time nobody was going to stop him.

4

On the Lam

For the first time in many months, John Picciano felt lighthearted. The bus had rolled into a breezy crisp Toronto day, the buildings were flashing in the sunlight. He strode through Queen's Park like a Texan, smiling at people, saying good morning to the old men on benches, breathing the sweet September air deeply. He could not remember when he had been so full of joy. He imagined himself a bull, charging and snorting around after being let out of the pen. He felt like a boy again, and if the park had been empty, he would have taken off skipping and hollering.

He was in that euphoric limbo between getting rid of one problem and waiting for another to come. Whatever lay ahead, this day, at least, was his. If he did not do anything but walk around the whole day, he wouldn't care. The Army, the war were far away. It was as though he had been born that morning. Every little thing he saw amazed

85

him. The leaves floating down to the grass, the way the clouds moved, the strong smell of tree bark and steaming hot dogs. This was the real world, not the dying one, and here he was at last, young, alive, and ready to partake of it.

The counselors at the Anti-Draft Programme were surprised to see him again and shocked when he told them that he had been deported. It turned out that John's counselor had inadvertently failed to warn him he should not reveal to Canadian immigration that he was AWOL. John was one of the first deserters the program had ever seen, and while they knew Canada was freely accepting draft evaders, the government had not yet taken an official position on whether to accept U.S. military deserters.

As it happened, Canada did not deal with the question of allowing deserters to become landed immigrants until almost two years later in the spring of 1969. By then thousands of deserters from all branches of the American armed services had made their way northward. Thousands were living underground in Canadian cities and thousands, like John, had been turned away at the border. Members of Canada's Parliament made a public issue of the obvious discrimination against deserters and moved to put them on the same footing as draft evaders and to accept them as prospective immigrants.

The antidraft counselors, apologetic and eager to help John, immediately found him a place to stay—a huge rickety attic studio in Toronto's West End which had become a way station for newly arrived draft dodgers. They all looked at John with curiosity and amusement, for they were used to seeing fellow refugees who had long hair, smoked dope, and belonged to the freak counterculture. Here was a new kind of maverick to the system—an ordinary GI, no different in style and attitude from a Dairy Queen counter boy.

"Hey, man," joked one dodger. "You're going to have to do something about that military haircut. Maybe you can tie each hair with twine and pull it out—*stretch* it."

John was given hearty meals, a mattress to sleep on, and moral support while he tried to piece out what his next step would be. The consensus at the attic commune was that he should try to get legal status to reside and work in Canada; the Anti-Draft Programme offered to hire a lawyer for him to defend his right in the courts to become an immigrant. But John decided he did not want to be made a test case; he had had enough of being used for one purpose or another, and besides, now that he had gained his freedom the hard way, he wasn't willing to risk losing it.

He decided to go as far away as possible. Clear across the continent in British Columbia, no one would know or care about who he was. There would be no danger of meeting the RCMP's, who had taken him into custody, or Canadian immigration men on the streets. No danger of being spotted by a traveler from Fort Dix or Lodi.

The Anti-Draft Programme offered to pay for his train ticket to Vancouver and insisted on leading him through back alleys to the station for "security's sake," a measure John found amusing considering he had walked off the Army base at Fort Dix in full view just days before. After hearing of John's deportation, the antidraft workers had become extra cautious and had persuaded him to stay out of sight, holed up in the commune.

After the stuffiness of the attic, he was glad finally to board the train, to stand between cars and lean out and catch the fresh air. There was a powerful sensation of movement under him as the train sped through the rocky countryside and the motion harmonized with the stirrings in his mind. He was going somewhere, moving out, for the first time in his life. All the frustrations of his growing years, the forces which had kept him down, seemed temporarily to slough off with the wind. Anything and everything seemed possible now, as though he had squeezed up out of a crevice and onto a peak with valleys on all sides just waiting to be explored.

"Hey, mister," John yelled to a tourist with Dallas baggage tags who was elbowing and shoving his way up to the front of the car. "Alberta's bigger than Texas!"

He knew he had been right. There were no more doubts in his mind that he had done the right thing. In fact, he had reached the point where he no longer felt afraid of those people who had thought and would think he had done wrong. He looked at the Texan with his smug, aggressive face. He felt like going over to him and telling him that he had just refused to go to a bad war. He felt like picking a fight with him. He didn't seem so big sitting down with his hat off; he looked small and childish. John thought back on his sergeants; they all seemed small and insignificant now. He could hardly remember what they looked like.

Not that he could see the future any more clearly. All he had to help him when he reached Vancouver was the name "Joe" and a single phone number which the antidraft counselors had scribbled on a piece of paper for him. What if it was the wrong number? What if the guy had moved or was out of town? John mused on how ironic it was that he should be miles away in another country, with only $200 and a phone number in his pocket, going clear across a continent he had never seen to a place where he knew no one. When he was a boy, the mere thought of having to leave home and travel outside Lodi had been enough to make him ill.

As he opened the car door to return to his seat, he caught his reflection in the glass and was pleased with it. He had a rather proud look. They could call him a coward, but he had nothing to be ashamed of. He was not running away from things so much as he was running toward them— toward a life that he could finally call his own.

When John reached Vancouver, he found that Joe existed. He answered the telephone, and as soon as John identified himself, he told him to call back on a different number at a public phone booth. It seemed that Joe, who was running an underground railway for American draft resisters from the Pacific Northwest and California, feared his telephone was tapped. The two met at a downtown café and Joe offered to put him up for a few days.

John set about immediately to carve out a new existence for himself. He had never been on his own before, nor had he really had the chance to tap his ingenuity. With the first flush of independence, his energies poured forth. The first task was to let his parents know that he was safe. He wrote them a long letter, made a duplicate, and arranged for two Canadian travelers to mail them from different cities in the United States so that he couldn't be traced. He tried to explain to his parents as best he could why he had finally done what they had tried so hard to persuade him not to do. He apologized for hurting them and urged them not to worry, that things would turn out all right.

He decided not to tell them his whereabouts in case the military authorities pressured them into revealing it. The most important thing to John was that he not get caught, that he not be forced through carelessness or stupidity to take a step backward. It was ironic that in the process of discovering who he was, he had to begin by being someone he wasn't. In order to build a future, he had to erase his past.

He got rid of everything that could identify him as John Picciano, fugitive from the U.S. military. He threw out his dog tags and burned letters he had received while in training. He wrapped up his military identification card, driver's license, birth certificate, and all other identification in a small bundle and hid it. He even clipped the name tags out of his shirts and underwear. He opened up a telephone book until he found a name which suited him—John Clark. It was common and innocuous and suggested nothing; with a name like that he wouldn't be typed and he could make the man behind it whatever he wanted. With the help of his friend Joe and other antidraft contacts, he got a Social Security card in that name and then a library card. He wrote out an imaginary biography of this new identity and memorized it. For several days he wrote the name over and over on a scratch pad and practiced telling his story aloud to Joe so that it would come naturally when he tested it for real.

After several days he decided he was ready. He knew he had to do things quickly, find a room of his own and a way to make a living. He had never felt so industrious. He rose at 6:30 A.M. so he could catch the first editions of the newspaper, comb the help wanted ads, and be at the door in time for the opening of business. He found it was hard for an unskilled American with only a high school education to find work in Canada, so he beat the pavement for days, checking out every factory and store that he passed, asking to wash dishes for a few dollars when he stopped to eat.

He finally got a job as a janitor in a hotel and found a room at a boardinghouse in downtown Vancouver, not far from East Georgia Street, where the city's wino population filled the sidewalks. The room was dreary with thin walls and dull furniture, a room which would have soon sent a man lonely or at odds with himself into a deep depression. John, however, did not mind it, for he was happy, all the internal confusion and conflict he experienced while in the military having subsided to give him peace of mind.

His new situation and his eager, excited mood made him ripe to meet a girl. His track record with women had not been distinguished. Throughout high school, he had been too shy to do much more than say hello to them and he feared that if he had ever made an all-out effort to woo one, he would have been sharply rejected. When he was graduated from high school, all he knew about love and sex was what he had read in the skin magazines.

His first real encounter with the opposite sex came that following summer. Her name was Charlene Esposito and she was regarded as the loosest girl in high school, the one the boys told all the stories about. John saw her at the grocery store while he was loading bags at a part-time job and she invited him to come up to her apartment after he finished. He accepted, his stomach fluttering.

She wore lime green short-shorts and her hair was piled on top of her head and she kept getting up to get John coffee or potato chips. Finally, she brought out some pictures of herself in just a bra and then some in no bra at all. She giggled as John looked through them, and he turned red and giggled slightly too, thinking how the guys had bragged about getting to her enormous boobies, and all the while she just had these little bitty ones. She must have worn falsies.

Charlene was sitting on his knee and rubbing his neck and he got very hot, but he was scared to death and his arms were like lead pipes, he couldn't move them. *God, would I love to lay her,* he thought.

Instead, he looked at his watch and jumped up, pretending that he had to go meet someone.

He brooded about the incident for days. He had made a fool of himself and passed up a chance of a lifetime. He had to try again. He called her up, but she said she didn't want to have anything to do with him and hung up. He couldn't sleep thinking about her, so he just kept trying and trying until finally she relented and invited him over.

It was a disaster. He was fine until they got into bed and he suddenly realized that he had no idea what he was doing. She kicked him out and never did speak to him again.

Now he was older. He had just turned twenty, no longer a teen-ager, and his act of desertion had changed him. He was bolder now, he felt, and readier to deal with women. He was eating lunch at a little Chinese restaurant near his boardinghouse one day when the opportunity fell in his lap. Two girls sitting in the next booth were talking about American draft resisters and how their group, the Young Socialists, had recently launched a campaign to help them out.

One of them was past thirty and slightly dumpy, but the other was tall, young and had long black hair. She talked fervently about raising money for Canadian antidraft support groups and speaking at rallies in behalf of the American resistance movement. There was nothing striking or beautiful about her, but she was very attractive and John decided she was not out of his league. He deliberated a few moments on what his move should be, whether he should temporarily abandon his new identity and revert back to being a fugitive. It might be unsafe, but that was the only way he could take advantage of the situation. He decided to do it part of the way and went over and introduced himself as a draft resister. That was all it took. The girl, whose name was Diane, had never met a real live resister before.

She began to come about three times a week to his place to make him dinner. They developed a light, well-rounded relationship. She put flowers in his room, washed and ironed his clothes, and generally gave him the caring for he needed at that time. Most important, with Diane he made the transition into manhood easily; their sex was excellent and she was a boost to his ego.

All things considered, he did not mind that her main interest in him seemed to be more or less as a collector's item. She enjoyed bringing him to the Young Socialist Club and telling her friends that she was going with an American exile. Their roles were clearly defined. She was the mothering lover and he was the wild wandering boy. He knew how to make her happy. He would roar at old ladies or break into bird shrieks just so she could get all excited, slap his hand, and say, "Oh, John, now stop that, you wicked thing!"

When he overheard someone at the club refer to him as "Diane's pet," however, he decided that enough was enough. From here on he would stay away from the club; it had been reckless of him to hang around a place which was probably watched by police anyway. He should have stuck to being straight John Clark. Having been a fugitive only six weeks, the FBI was bound to be looking for him and he figured he had probably been added to Canadian police lists as well, since he had been deported when he tried to seek legal residence in Toronto after his second AWOL.

John cooled his relationship with Diane, explaining that he still wanted to see her but that he needed to be on his own and to stay anonymous for the sake of safety. She was the only one he had told, besides his original contact, Joe, that he was not a draft resister but a deserter, living and working illegally in Canada, and he wanted to keep it that way. Since his border crossing, there had been reports of many more deserters trying to get into Canada; some of them had been turned away at the border and at least one other had been arrested in Toronto and deported.

He began to feel paranoiac about working at the hotel and finally quit, plagued by the fear that he had been traced there. For several weeks, he lived hand to mouth, getting the odd job here and there, nearly starving in between. For a week, he ate just one hamburger a day. One time, he went two days without food until the hunger pains got so severe he went into a restaurant and stuffed his pockets with crackers and bread. His shoes wore out, and although he devised an elaborate plan to steal from a five-and-dime store, he lost his nerve at the last minute. Eventually he scraped up enough money to buy a pair of Japanese ones on sale for $5.

He finally found a permanent job working in shipping and receiving at a wholesale textile company. It paid fairly well and gave him what he needed most, freedom from worrying about how he would keep himself alive, and the opportunity to live like a normal human being. He decided to give his life a strict order and put all his free time to constructive use. In a way, he felt as if he were on probation. He had to be a model citizen in order to make his desertion a positive instead of a negative act. If he made a wrong move or failed in some way, he felt it would somehow render what he did meaningless.

He became almost obsessively regular about everything he did. He came home straight from work, ate dinner at the same café every night, and spent the evening at the library, a place which gave him a nostalgic link to his previous life. The same smells of old books and waxed floors reminded him of his boyhood as he sat reading until closing time. He concentrated on the sociology section, taking an interest at one point in articles and books about the new computer age and the various methods people had devised to beat them. Occasionally, he would break the routine to spend an evening with Diane.

Part of the money saved with his simple and spare life-style he gave to Joe to use to help other draft evaders and deserters. But aside from that, he avoided becoming involved with the exile community. He did not frequent left-wing pubs or drinking spots where trouble was likely to break out and he steered clear of areas where drugs were traded or hippies hung out. He was so cautious and so aware of his fugitive status that he grew his hair, parted it a different way, and bought a new wardrobe of turtleneck jerseys and tailored slacks, a style of clothing that he had never been seen in before. The people he worked with knew him as John Clark, an American youth working in Canada. Whenever he was put on the spot and had to manufacture a story about his past; he would add it to the phony biography so he would be sure to tell the same story over again.

After several months, John began to get tired of the sameness of his existence. Although it had saved his sanity for a time, he knew he could be John Clark, warehouse worker by day and reader of library books by night, just so long. He was getting a bit homesick also and had an itch to see, if only for a while, his own country again. He packed his bags, paid his last rent bill, and set off for Seattle, Washington. He didn't stop to write a note to Diane. He would leave just as he came into her life, suddenly and without warning, like a blast of wind. It would probably be more romantic for her to remember him like that, anyway.

He had no trouble at the border—John Clark seemed believable enough for the American immigration man. He was glad to see the United States again, in spite of himself. He had missed things—a certain feel of life, the fast pace, the excitement, the enthusiasm of Americans, a Howard Johnson hot dog and a black cow. He had saved up enough money to just live and relax for a while, hiking in the hills outside Seattle, walking among the Douglas firs. He went to movies and concerts and made some friends in the Seattle antiwar groups, all the time watching for any sign that he was being followed or had been recognized.

John knew that it was just a temporary fling before he took another major turn in his life. He had been an outlaw for five months now, and he could stand it no longer.

In the past weeks it had really got to him. He had won his freedom at many different levels by deserting the U.S. Army; he had discovered what he was made of and a little bit about where he was going. But having gained that freedom, he had without question lost another. He was not free to live as a legal person with civil rights, police protection, and the right to travel wherever he wanted. He had come to feel as if he were wearing a black hat, like the bad cowboys in the movies. He was tired of sneaking around, of being constantly on his guard, of being afraid whenever someone tapped him on the shoulder to ask for the time or started up a conversation on a bus. Somehow, living so shiftily for so long a time had begun to diminish him in his own eyes. If he had made the right choice in what was probably the major decision of his life, then he should not have to hide it. He yearned to bring it out in the open, to announce to everyone what he was. In his particular predicament, his roots severed, with no stability and an uncertain future, he knew his worst enemy was inactivity and loss of self-respect. He knew he had to make a drastic change and the only thing left to do was to figure out what kind of change it would be.

The opportunity came one day in a coffee shop when he picked up a magazine and read a long feature article on the "Intrepid Four," sailors from the aircraft carrier, *Intrepid,* who had deserted ship in Japan four months earlier, in October, 1967. They had refused to return to active duty in the Tonkin Gulf where the *Intrepid*'s planes were bombing North Vietnam. With the help of a Japanese peace group, they had been taken to the Russian coast in a small boat and then flown to Moscow. From there they had gone to Sweden, which granted them "humanitarian asylum."

John was moved by some of the words they spoke at a press conference in Tokyo before their flight:

> You are looking at four deserters, four patriotic deserters from the United States Armed Forces. Throughout history, the name deserter has applied to cowards, traitors, and misfits. We are not concerned with categories or labels. We have reached the point where we must stand up for what we believe to be the truth. This overshadows the consequences imposed by the categories.
> Why have we done this?

We oppose the escalation of the Vietnam War because in our opinion the murder and needless slaughter of civilians through the systematic bombing of an agricultural, poverty-stricken country by a technological society is criminal.

We oppose the war as true Americans, not affiliated with any political party.

We believe that a majority of the people in Japan and the United States oppose the war in Vietnam, but are individually indifferent in taking actions to move toward peace. We appeal to the people of the world to realize that each one of us is responsible for the slaughter in Vietnam.

John thought about the Intrepid Four for several days. What they had done was a bit mind-blowing. It went far beyond his act of desertion or for that matter anything he had ever dreamed of doing. They had just walked off active duty, got help from the communists, and sought asylum in a country clear across the ocean. And they called themselves patriotic Americans. That was far different from skipping across a border with the intention of waiting out a war.

If he went to Sweden, he would really be going all the way. He could imagine how furious the people at the top of the U.S. military command must be with the Intrepid Four, with the Swedish government. It was the supreme insult, for a country that had a tradition of accepting political refugees from all over the world suddenly to be portrayed as casting out its own breed of dissenter onto faraway shores.

Any deserter who went to Sweden would probably never be able to come home.

Still, the thought of Sweden was intriguing. A new land. Beautiful blond girls. Europe—he had always dreamed of going someday. Sweden was socialist and it had no slums, no starvation. There was a lot of land and the streets were clean and uncrowded, the population small. He wondered if any other deserters had followed the sailors. He hadn't heard of any. If he went, perhaps he would be one of the first. At least he would have the freedom to say who he was. The Swedes had come out against the Vietnam War, had demonstrated against the U.S. embassy in Stockholm, and had held on their soil the Russell War Crimes Tribunal, which heard testimony about atrocities committed by Americans in Vietnam. An American deserter could hold his head up in Sweden.

John decided to take one last gamble. He had the money to get to Europe; but he didn't have a passport, and the only way he could get one was to go into the passport office and ask for it. It was risky—his name was probably on every black book in the nation. But he had to take the chance. In a way, it was a test of fate.

He flew to New York and applied for an American passport under his real name, presenting only his birth certificate. He told the officials he had got a last-minute acceptance at an English university and had to be there within a few days. The passport was granted in one day—with no questions asked. That night he drank a pint of Johnnie Walker, told his life story to an equally inebriated tourist from Boston, and caroused down Fifth Avenue until the wee hours of the morning. He didn't know what was more intoxicating: the liquor, the fact of having put one over on the system, or the feeling that somehow fate was on his side, telling him that he was right.

The next day he bought a New York *Times* and, through the haze of his hangover, found that the cheapest way to go abroad was by boat. It was also the safest as he figured if the passport office had found him out, the first place the police would check would be the passenger lists for Scandinavia-bound airlines.

As luck would have it, the *Cristoforo Colombo* was sailing for Naples the following day, and there was room for him to book passage. That was just fine, he thought. Everything was working out. He would blend in well. No one would be suspicious of an Italian-American taking a trip to Italy. It seemed fitting that he should be making this journey on an Italian liner, as though it was meant to be. He had always wanted to visit the land of his ancestors, although he never imagined it would be under these circumstances. It was ironic. Years before, his father had left Italy for the New World in hopes of a better life. Now he was fleeing his father's refuge, going back to the native land in search of his own freedom.

About twenty minutes before boarding time, John called his aunt in the Bronx to ask her to tell his parents about his departure. He did not feel strong enough to talk to them himself; it would be too painful. He might break down and backslide, as he had when they convinced him to go back to Fort Dix after his first two AWOL's. He knew how they must be suffering, how much he had hurt them.

His aunt squealed when she heard his voice. She was relieved and happy and filled him in on the family's doings. His parents had received visits from FBI men, who had tried to enlist their aid in locating John, but his father had cut them off both times, saying he did not know where his son was and had nothing more to tell them. They had stopped coming after the first two months. The two were bearing up well, but it had been hard and they missed John terribly. The aunt tried to convince John to stay and see them, but he said he had to leave immediately and she promised to explain his plans to them in the most optimistic terms possible.

As John leaned against the rails of the ship, he felt the stirrings of adventure, but they were muted. The water lapped gray at the sides and the ship shook as it blew its enormous whistles and cast off. A feeling of emptiness and loss settled over him. Right now his father must be working hard at the textile mill. The Cucuo twins were probably cruising down Main Street and Ken Barry might be ticking away the hours playing chess with himself. If he didn't fight the feeling, he might take a flying leap back onto the dock, back to Lodi, to warm kitchen smells, the sound of sawing in the basement.

It was too late to think such thoughts. The ship floated slowly past the Statue of Liberty, her figure looming high and majestic, veiled with a chalky-green patina. He looked down at his misshapen finger which had set wrong because the sergeant who broke it had warned him to stay away from the doctors. A smoggy mist was sweeping up the Narrows and over the Verrazano Bridge, moving in so low it almost covered the statue's crown. John thought of the words of welcome inscribed below:

> Give me your tired, your poor,
> Your huddled masses yearning to breathe free,
> The wretched refuse of your teeming shores,
> Send these, the homeless, tempest-tossed to me:
> I lift my lamp beside the golden door.

5

Going into Exile

It was dusk when the *Cristoforo Colombo* steamed into the blue Bay of Naples. Mount Vesuvius presided in the distance and frigates and destroyers from the U.S. Sixth Fleet displayed their strings of gay rigging lights, looking like pleasure yachts. John wandered through the narrow old streets, marveling at the swarm of people and small animals. These were a kind of Italian he had never known: raucous, bubbling over, fascinated with life. So different from the slow, tired citizens of Lodi who had left farm, sun, and fresh air to labor in the factories of New Jersey. He thought how much had been lost of their heritage on the journey over. His parents had never spoken Italian in the home and his father had talked only in vague terms about the poverty of his life as a boy on a peasant farm of Campobasso, which was not far from Naples in the Abruzzi e Molise region. What a grand history Italy had—from the Roman Empire to the Renaissance—and yet the Italian immigrant to America did not enjoy the same respect that a Frenchman or an Englishman did. John thought it odd, as he sat on the quay near the buttresses of Castel Nuovo munching warm *calzone,* how unaware he had been growing up of the history and traditions of his people. If someone had not told him once that Italians came from Italy, he might have thought his history began with Al Capone. The people of Lodi could say they had enough to eat now, he thought, but perhaps they didn't know what they had lost.

John resisted the urge to travel to Campobasso to search out a native Picciano. He could not afford to dally in a NATO country, so he caught the first train to Rome and then the Alpine Express bound for Scandinavia. The sea journey had been good to him; he was tanned and in fine health, feeling frisky and well nourished. Two American girls doing Europe sat down next to him and they chatted and drank beer together. Partly to impress them and partly to write one last chapter to the five-month imaginary odyssey of John Clark, he told them he was a wandering cabinetmaker just out of college.

The girls got off at Heidelberg. "Don't let the draft get you!" they yelled as they bid him good-bye.

Sweden, a land of rocks and forests and ghostly winter light, has traditionally been a neutral country. It is a member of neither the Warsaw Pact nor the North Atlantic Treaty Organization. Its government straddles between capitalism, with 90 percent of its wealth privately owned, and socialism, guaranteeing everyone health care, housing, and higher education. Sweden's neutrality became suspect in World War II, when it was accused of playing one side off on the other, staying out of the conflict while letting Nazi troops tramp across its territory. In the years after the war, some 500,000 immigrants from countries around the world sought a home in Sweden. Workers came from Italy, refugees from Yugoslavia and Hungary and, in the mid-fifties, objectors to France's Algerian War were even granted asylum. But in 1967, when deserters from the armed forces of the greatest power in the world suddenly landed on Sweden's doorstep, it was a whole new phenomenon.

The country's intellectuals, who found themselves continually called upon to explain or justify Sweden's neutrality in World War II, greeted such a prospect enthusiastically. A poll had recorded that approximately 83 percent of the Swedish population was against the war in Vietnam. What better way to take a stand, to scourge the nation of any lingering reputation of wobbliness, than to offer refuge to those who refused to fight in that war.

Ostensibly, the decision was billed as a humanitarian gesture. When deserters began trickling and then flooding in during late 1967 and early 1968, an informal policy was set up by which they could register with the police upon arrival and be given permission to remain without the government's formally granting them political asylum. The distinction slightly cushioned the blow to U.S.-Swedish relations but later served to anger the deserters, who found that it did not afford them enough protection from deportation.

John arrived in Stockholm in March, 1968. It seemed to him like a place out of a Hans Christian Andersen fairy tale. Islands and bridges and water everywhere. Bright colors in the stores. Green, red, yellow stucco houses. The Swedes were rejoicing in the coming of the spring, the reentry of the sun which in the deepest part of winter had come out for only six hours a day. The ice was breaking apart and jamming up in heavy floes. John felt peaceful and in harmony with it all.

Once again, he had only one name to contact for help—Hans Goran Franck, a Swedish lawyer who had been aiding American deserters since the *Intrepid* sailors arrived. Franck convinced an apprehensive John that he need have no fear of going to the police, for in Sweden the police were there to make things easier, not harder, for him. The two went down to the main station, John filled out several forms, and then Franck got him a room at the Swedish YMCA. To his surprise, John was told that he was not alone. Dozens more deserters had come to Sweden, many of them from Army bases in Germany.

"You've made a difficult and courageous decision," said one of the lawyers in Franck's office. He cautioned him: "You realize, of course, that the consequences would be great if you ever went back to your country. They would not forgive you quickly."

John moved in with a Norwegian communist who lived aboard a houseboat in the harbor. The Norwegian managed a coffee house called the Kafe Marx, a watering place for Swedish radicals and a handful of newly arrived deserters. For about three weeks, John helped wash dishes, rapped with fellow deserters about how messed up the military was, soaked up the fascinating foreign atmosphere of Stockholm, ate reindeer meat and korv (frankfurter) and Shrove Tuesday buns, and visited the royal ship *Vasa* several times. He wrote home about all of it. Then one day the Swedish Immigration Board informed him that a home away from home had been found for him with a left-wing Swedish family, Olof and Else-Marie Andersson, in Skälby, a residential town outside Stockholm.

Olof Andersson headed a lively family, part bohemian,

part ranch house suburban. He owned a sprawling modern L-shaped home, which housed one grandmother, a young daughter, a small son, and a bevy of Siamese cats skitting to and fro through the shrubs and patio garden. His wife, Else-Marie, a sturdy and handsome woman in baggy sweater and bare feet, spent her days constantly popping up and down to see to a pot or the cry of a child tangled in a coil of rope. The house was full of plants, a bright red piano matched by red doors, and some rather angry, brutal abstracts by Olof, a tall, slim man with sharp blue eyes and a small tapered beard the color of ripe wheat, who taught drawing and painting at a local junior high school.

Olof's life had been devoted to a study of socialism and he had made several trips to Cuba and Rumania to examine how far each had progressed in socialist forms of government. For years, he had been plagued by pangs of conscience about his life-style; it bothered him that he would curl up in his luxurious living room and listen to Beethoven on the stereo while people were being murdered in Vietnam. He was quick to tell you that he had built his house himself from a prefab kit, drank Vin Algérie Rouge, the cheapest, and ate beef only once every two weeks.

In late 1967 Olof had attended the Russell War Crimes Tribunal, sponsored by the aged philosopher Bertrand Russell, who had been too ill to make the journey from London to Sweden. The Swedish newspapers had lambasted the conference as communist propaganda. The Swedes thought America a great nation, its rescue of Europe from the Nazis had not been forgotten. Television, however, was beginning to bring the world another view, a glimpse into that same nation's activities in Indochina. Olof had had a closer look. He had seen the small Vietnamese boy, one of the few survivors in a village napalmed by American planes, who was brought before the tribunal. His eyes were like big black opals, and that was all you could see of his face, for it was as though covered by lava and the flesh on his arms and legs looked as if it had been boiled.

So several months later, when the Immigration Board asked the Anderssons if they would be willing to house a newly arrived deserter from America, Olof jumped at the chance. To him, John Picciano was someone who had defied the system in a way in which Olof never had and probably never would.

From the day he arrived, the Swedish Social Bureau had taken John and other deserters under its wing. He was treated as an immigrant and received his rent plus $18 per week for food and clothing, a sum which was guaranteed him for the first months until he got settled and working. The Anderssons gave him his board free so he had money left over. It was a relief for him to know that, after months of living on the edge of starvation, he would at least not go hungry.

About the time he moved in with the Anderssons, he got a distressed letter from his father.

"Your mother is feeling bad about this whole thing," it said. "Please, please do your family a service. Forget everything you've done. It's not too late. Please accept from me a ticket home."

John wrote back, telling him that he should not hold onto the hope that what had been done could be rectified. He would have to accept the idea of his son as an exile. There could be no going back. He tried to put a light touch to the letter, so they would believe that he was doing all right. "It's not so bad here," he wrote. "The food is great. As for the return ticket home, Dad, you don't need to waste the money. The American embassy, here, would be glad to pay my way back."

His father's letter made him sad and homesick; the Anderssons, with their bustling, close-knit style of life, caused him to be even more homesick. The first weeks of Sweden had been a time of inner revelry. He had basked in his freedom, felt light-footed, delighted in the fact that he could live openly, that he could introduce himself as a deserter and have people say with interested curiosity, "Oh, really?" as though he had said he was a parachute jumper or a glass blower.

But now the reality of his situation was beginning to hit him hard. He had done something which was probably irreversible. Sometimes it seemed so fantastic to him, as though he had had a long restless dream and suddenly awakened, in the middle of a strange country with no ties, roots, friends, prospects. His father had asked him to reverse the process. But that was impossible, unless he wanted to rot in some stockade. He was caught. Had he betrayed his family? They were probably sitting in their kitchen drinking strong tea, wondering what had become of their only son, what had happened to all those years. What if they fell ill? What could he do, how could he get to them?

It was strange being at the Anderssons, with their handmade pottery, bars of scented soap, wine, and silver table settings. It was strange to be suddenly surrounded by all this refinement. You could fit his parent's whole ground floor in the Anderssons' kitchen. He wondered if they had ever eaten with stainless steel on a plastic tablecloth. It was startling for him to get up in the morning to the sound of a Beethoven symphony filling the house like an orchestra, to walk into the living room in his bathrobe and find Olof buried in a thick book taking notes at his desk.

Realizing all this, the Anderssons went out of their way to make John one of the family, to build up his confidence, to help ease his feeling of disorientation. They brushed up on their English. Over and over, they tried to reassure him that what he had done was valid, that in his place they would have done the same thing. He would wander from room to room, aimlessly, not hearing what people said to him. Sometimes, in the middle of a conversation about food or the weather, he would interrupt, as if pressed.

"I've really burned all my bridges, now, Olof, haven't I?"

"We all have to burn bridges sometimes, John."

"Maybe I just couldn't take it. Maybe something's wrong with me; maybe that's at the bottom of it."

"Hey now! You must understand the larger view. There are people on your side. You are a victim of this murder and insanity your country is perpetrating in your name ... with your body if you had stayed. It doesn't matter that you couldn't take the Army. What matters is that you knew something was wrong; you refused to go along with it."

"I've let my parents down."

"In time, they will see that it was right. I would want my son to do what you did. Eat your dinner, now."

John did eat, and ate compulsively. He would down two helpings to everyone else's one and make excuses for it. He loved Swedish food. He loved Else-Marie's cooking. He needed to gain back the weight he had lost in Canada after deserting.

"No, no, John. You're getting too fat," said Olof, who was blessed with a Swedish lankiness.

"If you think I'm fat," said John, putting his arms out in front of him as if he were holding a bag of potatoes. "You should see my father. He's this fat."

John talked a lot about his childhood in Lodi, comparing it with the way the Anderssons lived. He became a child with them, and for a time, sensing his needs, they treated him the same way they treated their own children. He would bubble over, needing to talk to someone every moment of the day. He would follow Else-Marie around from the kitchen to the garden; he would be there when she made beds; he followed her to the store and once even into the bathroom until it dawned on him that she wanted to take a shower and he left with great embarrassment.

Else-Marie would find peace only when Olof came home and diverted John's attention. Sometimes even Olof would want to be left alone to do some schoolwork and would duck into his room and lock the door. Soon enough, there would be a knock and John would come bounding in, all hands, excited about some new idea or piece of news.

"Look at this!" he said, waving a copy of the Paris *Herald Tribune.* "A poll says Richard Nixon will be nominated at the Republican convention! That's going to ruin any chance I have of ever coming home!"

Then the two would talk about it for several hours and Olof's work would go undone.

The Anderssons knew that John's persistent garrulousness was necessary for the healing of his mind, knew that his incessant rattling on about unimportant as well as important matters was a way of releasing the anguish inside him. When they agreed to harbor a young refugee from a country whose youth was beginning to be torn apart by its military adventures, they knew that he would bring with him fresh wounds. They realized that they were providing a thin thread for him to hang onto and so they were patient and gentle. To Olof, the luxury of privacy paled in importance when set against the vision of a napalmed boy which had not left his mind.

Besides, the Anderssons were fond of John and touched by his gratitude. He would help Else-Marie with the housework, coach the children in English, and occasionally prepare a feast of Italian food for them. When they liked it, he would beam. John modeled himself after Olof. He asked to borrow his books and grew a little trimmed beard, just like Olof's.

They thought him highly intelligent, but secretly viewed him as typical of the working-class American, consumer-oriented, materialistic. They saw in him the characteristics of a class slightly bitter about its lot, watching with envy the life-style of the upper strata and wondering if it would ever be within reach. When they took him driving in their new car, John would invariably come up with the same series of remarks. "This is really a great car," he would say. "How much did it cost? Are they easy to get, how long would it take me to save up to buy one?"

Else-Marie and Olof tried every method and trick to get him out of his malaise, to lessen his dependence on them. They tried to get him out to meet people, but he would stay glued to the house, wary of leaving the security of the family atmosphere. They read him help wanted ads in the newspapers, but he would wave his hands deprecatingly, saying, "Those are bad jobs, I don't want bad jobs, I've had enough of them." And he would tell them of his work in warehouses and kitchens and as a supermarket carry-out boy. He wanted things to change, to begin again for him, he said. He couldn't just go on and on working bad jobs.

"Hey now! You know you aren't in the best of situations," Olof would say. "You could be in Vietnam. You have to work and work hard to make your way up."

"That's what my father said, and look at him. He's still just a factory worker."

So they abandoned the ads and tried to get John to learn Swedish. Olof presented him with a raft of language books, and whenever he was seen loitering or moping about, Olof would take him by the shoulders, slap a book down on the table, and say, "Study!"

John made a passing attempt; he learned some idioms, but his heart wasn't in it. The Anderssons urged him to try to assimilate and argued that he would continue to feel alienated as long as he remained physically inside, but psychologically outside, their culture. They recognized, however, that deep down John was having trouble admitting to himself that this was more than just a temporary stopping place and that he was probably here to stay for years and years. He felt closer to home speaking English, and somehow he did not want to learn their language because that would mean moving even farther away.

John's initial period of alienation was aggravated by the fact that he felt alone in his situation. The Anderssons lived a good hour outside Stockholm and he had little opportunity to meet other Americans. The deserter community, when he arrived, was small and had not yet coalesced. In the spring months, however, more fugitives filed into Sweden and by May, an estimated fifty had been given asylum.

Some were slipping out of American bases in West Germany and making their way to Sweden through underground networks in Germany, Holland and France. Some were coming in from Vietnam via Japan and the Soviet Union (although getting out of Nam was difficult for a GI), and still others made the journey from Canada and bases in the United States.

The first stirrings of an organized exile movement in Europe came in Paris in the winter of 1967–68. A group of resisters who had fled to France, which at that time was granting residence permits to draft dodgers and deserters although not officially accepting them, formed the French Union of American Deserters and Draft Resisters (FUADDR). Another group, committed to urging GI's to resist, formed Resistance Inside the Army (RITA) and published a newspaper called *ACT* that was distributed in U.S. military bases around Europe. Mailed to thousands of GI's, *ACT* urged them to "harass the brass by acts of political sabotage"—namely, holding peace demonstrations, putting up posters, committing acts of minor disobedience. The activity corresponded to a growing movement within the United States of on-base resistance, including GI coffeehouses and leafletting of bases.

By the spring of 1968, the deserters in Sweden, having spent the first few months of exile trying to get settled and adjust to the foreign environment, felt a strong need to organize themselves into a supportive union similar to the French Union of Deserters and Resisters. First of all, both Swedish and American newspapers had begun to take an interest in them. Reporters were prowling around, unearthing AWOL's here and there, sometimes ekeing statements out of unsuspecting, unworldly nineteen-year-olds not long away from the farms of Iowa or the Cumberland Mountains. The result was some bad press. It was decided that there would have to be official spokesmen to act as funnels for the barrage of reporters seeking stories on this newest antiwar phenomenon.

However, even if the press had not provided an excuse

for the deserters to form a group, there were other more vital reasons why they had to come together. They had a need to explain themselves, to define their actions. Most of the deserters were working-class or farm boys, unversed in politics. Most had been drafted, without knowing much about the resistance movement, or had joined the Army with patriotic ideas about being a soldier, seeing the world and serving their flag.

When, for one reason or another, their illusions were shattered, they reacted with a kind of crude, gut radicalism. They took dramatic, positive action which was hard for many of them to do, coming from families who resisted any form of change or departure from the norm. If they knew at bottom their instincts had been right, they did not possess the language or the intellectual sophistication to explain why. Thus, many of them in isolation in different parts of Stockholm or Göteborg and Malmö—two Southwestern seaport towns with easy access from Germany—were in a vague state of uneasiness. What had they done? Why exactly had they done it? It had all happened so fast.

They were secretly mad at themselves that they had gone into the Army in the first place. And they were angry at their parents for feeding them "a line of bullshit" about country and flag, for sending them off to die for no reason, for recklessly assuming that this war was like their war, a just and necessary one. They were angry at themselves for buying it all. If they had once questioned the bland assertion that the communists would be landing on American shores if they didn't go over and fight, they might not be spending their youth as refugees in a foreign country.

Such reflections provided no easy answers, and answers

were what all of them were desperate for. They had not thrown up their past and irrevocably altered their lives lightly. They were also in limbo between being one kind of person and becoming another and they needed to find a footing, a point of reference.

That rallying point became the American Deserters Committee. It was founded by a group of about fifteen deserters in Stockholm and the central figure in the organization was a man named Michael Vale, who had been asked by lawyer-supporter Hans Goran Franck to set up an organization in Sweden similar to the one in France. Vale, not an exile himself, was nevertheless a more powerful force than any deserter would have been able to be. He was more than a leader, or an organizer, or an ideologue. He was the closest thing to a high priest that the deserter community had.

Vale was in his middle thirties. Born into the silent generation which matured in the fifties, he became bored with the United States during his youth and left for Europe. He learned a half dozen languages and was a translator for several years. Then the Vietnam War and the exodus of young Americans from its grip came along and provided him with a more exciting and purposeful career. A committed socialist, he decided there was work to do among the deserters and so he made his way to Sweden.

Vale was a straight-looking character, short, energetic, with a sharp nose and a narrow jaw. He wore a pair of baggy corduroy trousers and a stretched-out turtleneck that hung loose as though it had been made for the neck of a bull. He often had a cold, but sick or well, he never stopped. It didn't matter what hour of the day or night, if there was someone who needed to talk or a hassle that had to be straightened out with the Swedish Social Bureau, Vale would be visible, running here and there, hands gesturing, shock of brown hair bouncing up and down.

He was generous and unsparing of his time. He opened his apartment to deserters and made sure that no one who was hard-up was without a meal and a place to sleep. At any one time, there were usually deserters sleeping in the hall, in the bathtub, in the kitchen, even in the crate-size storage stalls in the attic of Vale's apartment building. His home became a kind of seminary and his word was final. There were many who came to hate and fear him, but there was no one who did not regard him with a sense of awe.

He was a compelling, even magical, sort of person. But even if he had been less so, his effect would probably have been the same, for, in essence, he became what the exiles needed him to be. The Army had broken them down and it took a Michael Vale to build them back up again. The war had taken away their heroes and it was necessary, pressing, in fact, that they find new ones in order to believe again.

Vale gave them something to believe in—themselves. A Trotskyite, he disliked the United States and the Soviet Union equally, denouncing the capitalists and warmongers in the former and the bureaucrats and the Stalinists of the latter. Vale believed in the perfectibility of the working-man and that, to him, was the only "correct line" of thinking. While the parents and friends of many of the deserters were telling them they were traitors, cowards, good-for-nothings, Vale assured them that they were men of courage, that history would judge them well. He was eloquent, articulate, and witty. He taught those whose educations barely skimmed the Bolshevik Revolution and ignored Marx and Engels that they were the salt of the earth. The heroes of the revolution. He taught them about the Third World, that even though their own people thought them no good, there were millions of Vietnamese peasants, Cuban communists, black liberationists who considered them the vanguard of the armies of freedom in America. Since they felt depressed and cast out them-selves, it was easy for the new exiles to understand oppression in the Third World. It was a kind of basic training, being part of the ADC with Vale. He infused his disciples with confidence; his own self-assurance bubbled over onto them. If it had not been for him, many would have probably gone to seed in their loneliness, turned to drugs or bumming.

The deserters who made up the ADC in its early days were an eclectic group. Although primarily working class, there were also boys from liberal middle-class families who had finished college only to be drafted. There were Roman Catholic boys from small Western towns who had ended up as sergeants in Vietnam and after killing a few "gooks" had lost their stomach for it. There were Jewish boys, sons of shopkeepers in the big cities, who caught the winds of the antiwar movement through their city friends and city papers and left the Army almost as soon as they got in, GI's who came from a line of clergymen and just missed getting CO status, high school dropouts who joined the Navy, high achievers who were assigned to Special Forces train-ing units in Germany and taught counterinsurgency tac-tics in preparation for tours in Indochina, young men who had to take a year off from college to earn their tuition and who somehow could not get their draft board to extend their student deferments, blacks who had suffered discrimination in U.S. bases in Germany.

At the core of the ADC was Vale's front man, Bill Jones, a tall, lean boy from St. Louis who had been trained as a combat medic and deserted from Germany when his name came up among the large lists of Vietnam-bound GI's that were being levied from the German bases. Jones, a former seminarian who came from a wealthy Roman Catholic family, had considerable intellectual prowess and seemed to exist on a plane slightly removed from the rest. He was an aloof fellow who shied away from close friendships and slipped easily into the role of chief ADC spokesman, a kind of deserter figurehead for an organization run by Vale. George Carrano, twenty-five, a draft dodger who had graduated from City College of New York with a major in history, became Vale's deputy and the second brain behind the committee. George was the first draft resister accepted by Sweden and one of the few who chose the Scandinavian nation over Canada, which absorbed the bulk of the draft dodgers during the war years. George's father was a retired Army colonel who, after many months of anguish and reproach, came around to supporting his son.

In the late spring of 1968, a large second batch of deserters came into Sweden, many of them having fled Southeast Asia with the help of the Japanese antiwar group, *Beheiren*. Among them was Mark Shapiro, a twenty-two-year-old Jewish Vietnam veteran who had seen his best friend shot beside him and decided there wasn't any reason for his friend to have died. Mark had spent about six months underground in the Orient and by the time he reached Stockholm he was exhausted and depressed. He was an average-looking Midwesterner with short dark hair, thick glasses, and a muscular frame. His background was middle class; his mother, the manager of a store in St. Paul, Minnesota. He was anxious about his future and frustrated that he had been unable to get a college degree before the war came along and cast him adrift.

Like John Picciano, Mark Shapiro was temporarily embittered by the lot fate had assigned him. When the two met, they hit it off immediately. Being in Sweden, they both agreed, was no adventure abroad—it was a frightening nightmare. Mark, who lived in the center of Stockholm, told John about the American Deserters Committee. John's initial reaction was cynical. All that political rhetoric—capitalist pigs, worker's control, seizure of power, the Third World.

"Oh, come on, what crap," said John, who mused on how Chickie and Dan Cucuo and the rest of the guys in Lodi would have snickered. That sort of stuff was for commies or bookworms with thick glasses.

Mark worked on him, however. If nothing else, the ADC was a place to meet people, Mark said. John reluctantly unglued himself from the Anderssons' living room and, to his surprise, began enjoying the ADC meetings. Mark and John became fast friends and they immersed themselves in ADC work, John little by little gaining an understanding of Vale's leftist politics, learning the jargon, and getting turned on by the ideas.

The two were alike in many ways. They soaked up the thinking of the counterculture without taking on its social trademarks. They steered clear of drugs, both hard and soft, because they thought it was difficult enough to "get it together" without scrambling up their brains all over again. They also disliked drinking, fearing a loss of control. They refused to grow their hair long because they hated the way it itched and shunned hip clothes for the shirts and slacks they'd worn back in high school. Mark sported two-tone shoes which had a look of the fifties and John felt secretly uncomfortable when he saw the American flag worn on somebody's back. They took some ragging for being too straight, but that strengthened the bond between them.

John looked up to Mark, who came from a slightly higher social stratum. Mark, who considered a college degree a sign of status, helped plant the desire in John's mind for a university education, a desire that was to grow later until it became a near obsession. The two spent hours together, talking about radical politics, about what their individual acts of desertion had meant. They would often be seen walking by the water on the Strandvägen, their identical heavy winter coats flapping in the icy north wind. Some called them Tweedledee and Tweedledum.

As John got to know other deserters and became a part of the community, his view of himself underwent a change. He no longer considered himself so different from everyone else. He was no longer a misfit, forging along on some alien plane, far removed from the one on which normal people existed. Suddenly he was among people who had, in one way or another, always stood apart from their peers. He was among men who had been unwilling, unable, to ride along through life, taking what came, for better or worse. For perhaps the first time in his life, he saw that there was another world, a world where people talked enthusiastically about serious ideas, and were unembarrassed about trying to discover who they were and where they were going. In a way, it was like seeing different parts of his experience personified. There was Mark, who had resented the lousy teachers and the lousy education he had gotten back home; there was Bill, who had felt used, and George, who was sensitive and sincere and unafraid to show it.

As far as the Anderssons were concerned, by summertime John had turned a corner and they could heave a sigh of relief. He had grown out of his childish dependence on them. He had become calmer and stronger and had lost his need to talk a blue streak. He no longer expressed doubts about his desertion, no longer needed reassurance from Olof.

Reconciled to the fact that Sweden would be his home for a long time to come, he studied Swedish in earnest. Knowing that John could understand what they said, the Anderssons went back to conversing in their native tongue.

6

Breaking the Sword

The American Deserters Committee was started in late February, 1968, and on March 15 a press conference was called to announce its formation and to denounce the Criminal Intelligence Division (CID) of the U.S. Army for what the ADC considered its subversion of Roy Ray Jones, the first deserter to arrive in Sweden. Jones, a black from Detroit, Michigan, had fled from Germany and slipped into Sweden unheralded in the summer of 1967, several months before the well-publicized Intrepid Four. Swedish officials, sympathetic to his stories of discrimination and brutality at his U.S. base in Germany, granted him permission to stay but kept it quiet. In early 1968, however, Jones, living in Malmö, where a substantial deserter community had not yet surfaced, received several visits from what was thought to be a CID agent and was finally persuaded to return to his unit. The ADC claimed that threats and harassment had been used, a charge which Jones later confirmed.

The committee set out to provide a forum for the growing collection of exiles to tell their stories and also to send out word to other discontented GI's that if they decided to desert, they would not have to go it alone—there was a group that would help them when they reached Sweden, find them housing, jobs and a fresh start.

The ADC was intent on giving a political definition to the act of resistance. On April 3, they gave another press conference to read a charter statement which said in part:

> With each new day dissent against the war in Vietnam grows. Demonstrations and protest marches occur in Washington, New York, Paris and throughout the world. Eminent doctors, philosophers, and scientists voice their dissent in public speeches. And still the escalation continues. Every month the draft quota grows, more and more troops are sent to fight and die in the most brutally oppressive war of our times. Protest seems to bounce harmlessly off the walls of the Pentagon. . . .
>
> The only way to stop this war seems to be for everyone who can be used in its continuation to refuse at all costs to contribute to this madness. . . .
>
> We, ex-soldiers, who have come to Sweden, have done just that. We have refused to participate in any way with an organization which carries on all the death and destruction in Vietnam. We choose to live in exile rather than be used as pawns in the deadly game of imperialism. We found that our duty to the rest of mankind and to the Vietnamese people far outweighed our duty to the U.S. Army. A choice of loyalties had to be made. We chose to be loyal to our fellow men and therefore to ourselves.
>
> And each day more men come to Sweden, motivated by the same loyalty, and for each man that comes, there is one less man that can be used for the futile aggression in Vietnam.

The ADC began publishing a magazine called *The Second Front* which was circulated in Sweden and France and found its way to England, Holland, and other countries where deserters were being harbored or were in hiding. The Committee also put out a four-page newspaper, the *Second Front Review,* for distribution on U.S. military bases throughout Europe. Originally started in Paris, the bulletin carried personal stories by deserters, letters from GI's resisting inside the Army, poems, instructions on how to desert, and lists of contacts and committees set up in European capitals to assist deserters. Its motto was: "Be a man, not a war machine. Desert." One issue, in September, 1968, contained a column headed "Words of Wisdom" and below, a quote from President Lyndon Baines Johnson: "I hate war. And if the day ever comes when my vote must be cast to send your boy to the trenches, that day Lyndon Johnson will leave his senate seat to join him."—Campaign for U.S. Senate, Texas, 1941.

While the ADC did political organizing, sympathetic Swedish groups took over the burden of helping procure social services for the deserters. The Swedish government had publicly registered its feelings about the Vietnam War. The U.S. ambassador, William W. Heath, could not speak or be seen publicly without being shouted down or pelted by tomatoes. Olaf Palme, then Education Minister and later Prime Minister, had marched in an antiwar parade arm in arm with a North Vietnamese diplomat. The action had so enraged Johnson that he ordered the recall of Heath in the spring of 1968 and the U.S. embassy in Stockholm remained without a diplomatic chief for nearly two years until President Nixon appointed Jerome Holland in early 1970.

Thus, it was not surprising that the ADC's main Swedish support group was the Swedish Vietnam Committee—an organization of the nation's ruling Social Democratic Party. The committee, which consisted of Members of Parliament and prominent professors and lawyers, including Hans Goran Franck, sponsored annual conferences on Vietnam, and raised money for medical supplies to be sent to Hanoi. The other major support organization was the FNL (Front for National Liberation), a coalition of more radical Swedish left groups which had raised close to $1,000,000 for the North Vietnamese to spend any way they wanted.

The FNL provided the most practical aid to the exile community. It set up a special eight-man deserters' committee that acted as a liaison between the Swedish Social Bureau and the deserters. The committee often found lawyers for individual cases, helped set up and publicize speaking tours for the ADC, and kept a steady flow of money coming in through fund-raising drives.

On July 4, 1968, the ADC descended on the U.S. embassy. About 200 American tourists, as well as the embassy staff—diplomats in blue suits, clerks in brown, and secretaries in bright flowered dresses—had gathered on the lawn to picnic and pay homage to the flag.

The ADC had carefully planned the demonstration, which was geared to denounce the newly begun Paris peace talks as a farce. It was decided that the most effective form of protest would be a kind of low-key guerrilla theater action. They would infiltrate the tranquil Sunday ceremonies on the spacious grounds of the embassy—a miniature estate of glass and steel just outside the city—and occupy the flagpole.

The deserters had arrived well before the ceremony got

under way. Their presence—most wore jeans and combat gear, except for John, who had put on his one suit to mark the occasion—did not go unnoticed. By the time the ambassador climbed onto the podium, there were about 150 Swedish police with eight paddy wagons in sight. As the band struck up the national anthem, a dozen deserters quietly sat down around the flagpole, near the ambassador's podium, and began to chant antiwar slogans.

The singing faltered. The marine honor guard looked confused. A few ladies gasped and their career diplomat husbands muttered expressions of outrage. Chaos was unleashed. The police moved in and started to grab the squatters, some of whom responded by spitting up at the flag.

George Carrano, who had been standing on the sidelines with John handing out leaflets, jumped up and yelled, "U.S. out of Vietnam!" He was dragged away by a policeman and John defiantly echoed the shout, whereupon another policeman, who barely reached John's chin, grabbed him around the neck from behind, twisted back his arm and lifted him off the ground. John, gagging, lost his balance, and the two fell backward in a heap, John on top.

In the paddy wagon on the way to jail the policeman was apologetic. "I'm sorry I have to do this," he told John and George. "I want you to know I'm sympathetic to you."

Mark Shapiro, Bill Jones, George, and John spent the night in jail. A few weeks later they were tried on charges of disrupting a public meeting. George was also charged with "insulting the representative of a foreign state" and John with resisting arrest.

The FNL, which had publicized the trial as a political one, filled the courtroom. The judge decided he wanted to

see just what had taken place when John had resisted
arrest. The short policeman, looking rather embarrassed,
tried to duplicate his armlock on John. He strained and
pulled, but to no avail. He could not lift John off the
ground. The courtroom erupted in laughter. The charge
was dismissed, but the judge found all five guilty of
disrupting a public meeting. George was fined $200, John
$100, and the others $50 each.

John was rather proud of the whole thing. "It makes you
high on the power of your own act," he remarked to
another deserter. He wrote home about it, enclosing pictures of the demonstration that appeared in the Stockholm
newspapers.

His father was less pleased. He replied by return mail:
"Don't get involved. It's not good."

The U.S. embassy, for its own part, was not exactly an
innocent victim. A figure often seen entering and leaving
its great echoing halls was one William Russell, the civilian
editor of the military newspaper *The Army Times* and the
one who had got Ray Jones to give himself up. Since the
Jones case, word had spread that Russell had approached
other deserters with similar proposals. It seemed he would
offer a special deal: If a deserter agreed to return to his unit
quietly, without press conferences, without alluding to his
motivation or to Vietnam, he would get off lightly with a
few months in the stockade. If the deserter were to
denounce the ADC and repent his straying from the path,
he could expect even more leniency. On the other hand,
the alternative was not nice. If and when the deserter *did*
decide to go home, there would be no mercy. According to
those he approached, Russell was an enthusiast who spared
no effort to succeed in his missions. He arranged for the
parents of at least one exile to telephone their son, at Army

expense, and urge him to cooperate so he could come home.

The ADC, in turn, arranged for Russell's Waterloo. Vale and George Carrano obtained a room in the Jerum dormitory at the University of Stockholm, equipped it with tape recorders and hidden cameras, and had a deserter put in a call to Russell, who was staying somewhere in Stockholm. Russell soon arrived at the dormitory, and the Army editor was caught in the act, tapes spinning and cameras clicking as he was offering his deal. The encounter was splashed in the newspapers. Several members of the American embassy subsequently were sent home and Russell was never seen in Sweden again.

After the "Jerum Affair," as it was called, the embassy assumed a more passive role as far as the deserter scene was concerned. A high consulate official confided several months later that the staff had become almost paranoiac about calls from deserters.

"We never could be sure if a deserter called us, what he was up to. If someone calls me now and says, 'I think I want to give myself up. Will you meet me at a bar and we can talk about it?' I refuse. I tell them they have to come to me. Once they're here, on my territory, I can do something for them. And they can't accuse me of trying to come after them to seduce them."

"You might call it protection against 'Russell-rustlers,' " he said.

Whatever new aboveboard policies the embassy followed after the Jerum Affair, it did not necessarily mean that the Army CID or other American agencies subscribed. Deserters would complain of being followed, of receiving strange phone calls. Every once in a while a new person, claiming to have deserted, would show up at

ADC meetings and, after a few weeks, suddenly disappear. Usually these people would act like superhippies or talk Stalinist politics too abrasive to be believed. The ADC consequently made a practice of watching a newcomer closely, testing him on his story, listening for the slip which would reveal him as a straight pretending to be a freak.

Even the Swedish police were suspect. More than one deserter was surprised when he walked into the police station to register several weeks after arriving and found the police chief knew his name before he had even given it.

Mark and John had one encounter with what they thought were small-time police informers. It was reminiscent of a Keystone Kops comedy. For several days, Mark had noticed the same old man with a cane and thick overcoat hanging around his apartment building and the same Mercedes Benz parked down the road. When John and he came out and found him there one afternoon, Mark decided to call his bluff.

"Watch this," he whispered to John and took out his camera and began snapping pictures.

The man flailed forth with his cane, aiming at the camera and beating Mark in the process. The pair took off toward the tunnelbana—the Swedish subway—and as they were running down the stairs, an old lady pointed them out to the Mercedes driver, who got out and followed them, picking up a partner on the way. It took John and Mark two tunnelbana changes and a bus ride to lose them. Later Mark went away for a few days, and when he got home, his apartment had been burglarized. The only thing taken was the camera, complete with film. The following week, John recognized the Mercedes driver leaving a Stockholm police station.

By late summer John had assumed a major role in the ADC. He traveled around Sweden making speeches, often acting as a liaison between Swedish officials and the deserters. The ADC had given him more than an identity. It had provided him with a direction for his abilities, an outlet for his creative instincts. He had felt a sense of achievement and intellectual excitement in school only once that he could remember—in a history course when he debated his classmates right under the table. Now it was as though the good things that happened to him in that class were magnified a hundred times.

John made a trip to the small northern town of Lindesberg to scout out the possibilities for jobs and housing for deserters. With the constant influx of new exiles—by the end of 1968 there were about 200—the ADC was trying to find new areas where they could settle. The most difficult logistical problem the deserters faced was finding living quarters. There was a housing shortage in Stockholm and places for single men were in especially short supply. The shopkeepers and landladies of Lindesberg, however, expressed polite apprehension at the prospect of an invasion by military deserters with long hair and funny clothes. John went back and persuaded the ADC to abandon the idea of establishing deserter colonies in the smaller towns since they tended to be less liberal and more cliquish than the larger cities.

In August the ADC was invited to send delegates to the annual International Communist Youth Festival and John, Mark, Bill Jones, and a few other deserters chosen to represent the committee set off for Sofia, Bulgaria.

The festival was like a giant circus. In addition to seminars, meetings, panels, and rallies, there were parades and sports events—everything from skydiving to high jumping and underwater diving. It all looked so normal, as if it had been a giant gathering of students organized by the United Nations. In the morning the delegates were awakened by Swiss trumpeters.

Settled in his hotel, bedecked with flags and banners, John marveled. Here he was, a small-town boy from New Jersey who in his childhood had never been farther away from home than New York City, behind the Iron Curtain with throngs of communist leaders from all over the world, East and West, at an extravaganza as spectacular as the Olympics.

He was fascinated with being in an East European city. Skipping some of the minor meetings, he set about to find the little old man and lady huddled beside their wireless that he had seen on the Radio Free Europe television commercials back home. He always had wondered what happened to them after the guards burst through the door, smashed their radio, and dragged them off. He rode around on the trolleys, stopped into cafés, and made several English-speaking friends, asking the same questions of all of them: Are you arrested if you speak against your government; can you choose the job you want or are you assigned one; can you ever leave the country for a vacation?

The Bulgarians laughed at him. John found out propaganda was propaganda, no matter where you go. The majority liked their system of government, remembering the poverty and injustice before socialism. They had good clothes, enough to eat, and they lived well; they were given exit visas in many cases to visit neighboring countries, including Austria and Italy. But, they asked, what about America? Were people really starving in the ghettos of the big cities? Were people really left to die if they didn't have enough money to go to a hospital? Were they murdered just walking in the streets?

The young American communists at the conference told the exiles the latest news from the States, the price of hamburgers, the new fads, the state of the antiwar movement, which was gaining momentum, and the despair that had settled over young America after the assassinations of Martin Luther King and Robert Kennedy earlier in the year.

"Everything's fucked up," one youth told John. "You don't want to go back. You're better off making a life for yourself over here."

Friction between the deserters and other delegations developed early in the seven-day conference. It seemed the Americans, as well as the Russians, became unnerved by the deserter representatives' stridency and harsh political lines. At one point, Bill Jones, taking a Maoist line, had accused the Soviet Union of revisionism.

Being slightly ahead of their time in cultural habits, the deserters also looked strange to the other delegations. Some wore shoulder-length hair, headbands, and wild clothes. Moreover, claimed one middle-aged American communist, they were full of unreconstructed energy and unchanneled anger. They were accused of throwing their weight around, shooting off at the mouth, and rapping their silverware on the table in protest against one resolution or another.

But then the deserters were in a different category from the scholarly Marxist thinkers from Chicago and New York who led normal middle-class lives and wrote treatises on the politics of resistance. The deserters were living those politics. It was all they had. They didn't work for the revolution; they *were* the revolution. Creating a colorful splash and being controversial at the conference might have been a way of demanding that the musty, theoretical Marxists acknowledge that fact.

In any case, John, who had been more interested in touring Sofia than having polemical battles at the round tables, stepped in to mend some fences—primarily because he looked straighter and talked a politically softer line than his intense comrades. Delegates were particularly interested in knowing why there were so many reports that deserters took drugs. John tried to explain that some of the deserters, like hundreds of other GI's, had come out of Vietnam with bad drug habits largely because the Army almost totally ignored the widespread drug use there. The communists wondered how revolutionaries could be drug addicts.

A meeting with representatives from North Vietnam—the most poignant experience of the seven-day conference—brought everyone together, however, and petty squabbles were forgotten. The Vietnamese officials were gracious and low-key. They showed pictures of napalmed villages, burned children, and then, the most dramatic photographs of all, shots of several hospitals in different parts of North Vietnam that had been leveled by bombs. At first, John was incredulous. He did not believe the North Vietnamese. It had to be propaganda. The United States would never authorize the bombing of hospitals. That was absurd; besides, what would they gain by it?

The North Vietnamese explained the strategy of terror bombing, of trying to destroy the enemy's morale. John finally believed them. The pictures were real. Hospital beds and broken equipment could be seen in the rubble and there were nurses who had come to testify. Someone had to be responsible. The North Vietnamese didn't bomb themselves. Such direct repeated hits could only have been deliberate.*

John felt sick inside. He felt ashamed to be an American. He remembered back in his childhood when the television stations signed off for the night with the national anthem, against a background of planes roaring in the sky. It hadn't meant anything to him then. But now it came home to him, seeing the pictures of the seared children, of hospitals obliterated, just what those jet fighter planes meant. He thought of the immense power of the United States and what it could do. A strong feeling of personal responsibility gripped him. How could he ever make it up to these people, to their children, their grandchildren?

John was amazed at the calm attitude of the North Vietnamese. If he were in their place, he thought, he would want to kill every American he saw, no matter who it was. And yet they treated the American delegations, especially the deserters, with warmth and deference. They gave each deserter a white flower and a peace ring made out of aluminum from a shot-down American bomber.

"You are a hero. You did not go to Vietnam and so one more of our people lived. You are a hero of the war," one Vietnamese official said to John.

It struck him as ironic. People in the United States were calling him a traitor. Now he was cast a hero. And in reality he knew he was neither. "Thank you," John replied and took the gifts. "But I'm not a hero at all, you know."

---

* This was in the summer of 1968. In August, 1973, three Air Force veterans told the Senate Armed Services Committee that they "routinely selected enemy hospitals and suspected hospital sites as targets" to bomb in North and South Vietnam (New York Times, August 9, 1973, p. 1).

After the conference, John took a long train ride through Eastern Europe, stopping off in Hungary, East Germany, and Czechoslovakia. The atmosphere in Prague was tense. It was just a few days before the Soviet invasion and the streets seemed strangely quiet, as though people had gone inside and shut their doors. There had been an uneasiness between the Czech and Soviet delegates at the conference, and toward the end the Czechs had refused to participate in conference activities, in protest against Russian moves to stamp out freedom in their country. They raised the Czech flag outside their window and gathered each morning in front of the main building to sing their national anthem. One delegate confided sadly to John that he thought the Soviet Union would, in the end, "roll right over us."

In East Berlin, John noticed that the shelves in the stores were somewhat sparse, and as in Prague, the streets looked half-empty. But the people he did see were friendly and he was particularly impressed with the police, who seemed more humane, more like people, than walking uniforms. They helped old ladies across the street and gave children piggyback rides. He saw one drunk take a swing at a policeman who did nothing but scold him and shoo him on his way.

John returned to Stockholm to find the deserter community in chaos. Forces were gathering against Vale. The ADC leader had always been secretly sniped at for being intolerant of any "incorrect" form of thinking. But by the fall of 1968 he was accused of everything from character assassination to being an *agent provocateur* for the CID.

The problem with Michael Vale was that if one did not agree with him and said so, he would be sharp and sarcastic. He was given to contemptuous bursts of anger and he had a way of making his victims look like fools. Once he grabbed a copy of *Newsweek* out of the hands of one deserter, threw it into the wastebasket, and told him to stop fiddling around with trash and start reading Trotsky.

Many of the deserters began resenting his dictatorial attitudes. "It's like a kindergarten around here," said one person who had been berated by Vale. "It's the Army all over again." "You've got to admire him, though," said another. "He's like a Rasputin and he's got a technique. He browbeats new guys for the first few days and then lets up and they end up loving him because it feels good when you stop banging your head against the wall."

"Yeah, you've got to admire him . . . like you admire the work of a butcher."

Vale also had a falling out with the Swedish Vietnam Committee over his hard-line politics. The committee, being closely aligned with the government, took issue with the ADC's militant stands. The committee's chairman, Bertil Svanstrom, a prominent Swedish liberal who later received the Soviet Union's Lenin Peace Prize, was particularly vociferous about the embarrassment that the ADC's pro-Vietcong stand was causing to Sweden. He criticized the *Second Front Review* for encouraging desertion and publicizing Sweden as a haven and argued that if the deserters kept a lower profile, the government would be able to do more for them. Vale launched a strong counterattack. The political dispute between the two degenerated into a personality issue. Suddenly, there were rumors that Svanstrom had a "pro-Nazi background" as a foreign correspondent in Berlin during World War II.

In the midst of the battle, the good name of Hans Goran Franck, the man who had been responsible for getting deserter after deserter admitted to Sweden, also suffered.

Franck, a member of Svanstrom's committee, refused to side with Vale and suddenly it was rumored that Franck was untrustworthy.

"I would not be surprised," said one disgruntled friend of Svanstrom's, "if Vale was either working for the Ford Foundation or collecting checks from the U.S. Government."

Throughout all the backbiting and infighting, Vale still had loyalists who staunchly defended him. If his tactics were harsh, they said, it was because he was passionately dedicated to seeing the ADC survive as a strong organization that had influence within Sweden and indirectly on U.S. Vietnam policies. Who else could have brought together such a hodgepodge, who else could have persuaded a $300 per week computer analyst and a farm boy on relief to work together for the same aim? Without him, there would have been no exile community, the deserters would have been scattered, anonymous, and powerless; they would have been unable to affect the course of the war and their individual acts would be stripped of a larger significance. If Vale didn't keep a tight rein on the ADC, his supporters argued, it might fall into the wrong hands.

Vale's opponents, however, decided that that was exactly what had happened. Mostly boys from middle- and upper-middle-class backgrounds who were more literary than political, more liberal than militant, they did not particularly identify with the working-class hero ethic propounded by Vale. Although they agreed with the theory of class struggle and decried repression, racism, and imperialism in America, they thought Vale and the ADC hard liners laid it on a little too heavily.

A few were pacifists who were against all wars rather

than just the Vietnam War. Others were basically apolitical, contending that it was "politics" that had created Vietnam and got them into the mess in the first place. All of them felt that the ADC was doing nothing constructive for the individual deserter and had concentrated too much on political gestures of questionable value at the expense of the social needs of the community.

Moreover, they were tired of the ADC rumor mill, of the paranoia of being called counterrevolutionaries and reactionaries, of being told to shuck off their "bourgeois hang-ups." The last straw came when a deserter from Georgia, George Meals, clashed with a black deserter, who accused George of calling him "nigger." George was subsequently expelled from the ADC for being a "racist."

"Wow, with friends like this, I don't need enemies," said a shaken George after the incident.

In October, he and about a dozen other deserters decided to split and form their own organization—the Underground Railroad. Emphasizing the humanitarian rather than the political needs of the community, it geared itself to helping deserters with the day-to-day problems of being stateless persons. The Railroad members came to the aid of individual deserters, who at that point were entering Sweden at the rate of about ten to fifteen a week. While tackling the recurring logistic problems of living accommodations, jobs, and schooling, they also began delving into other aspects of the exile experience. With the help of Dr. Robert Rommel, an American psychologist who was then teaching at the Swedish Institute, a program of sensitivity training was started to explore the psychological effects of exile. They published a journal called the *Internal Hemorrhage,* which concentrated on counterculture lifestyles, printed health food recipes, poems, short stories and attacks on the ADC. At one point the Railroad, which included a few musicians, experimented with starting up a band.

It was as important to the Railroad group to interpret the act of desertion and its aftermath in philosophical and literary terms as it was to Vale's "working-class" followers to put it into a social and political context. George Meals was representative of this other deserter experience, the kind that befell the sons of the merchants, the doctors and lawyers, the bankers of America.

George was a tall, well-built chap with a wispy black beard and deep, lazy brown eyes. A native of Atlanta's gracious Peachtree Street, he had a deferential manner and a habit of leaning back in his chair and sliding his glasses down on his nose so those he was talking to were unable to see what his eyes were doing. He was inclined to the poetic, lacing his conversation with metaphors and pithy asides. George came from a middle-class family; his father was a wholesale hospital supplier. He readily admitted he was weaned on a silver spoon, as he liked to describe it, whereas the John Piccianos of the community had grown up on a popsicle stick. He did not feel guilty about it; it was just a fact of life. True, it had given him a slight advantage, but the advantage had not been great enough, in the end, to buy him a ticket off the Vietnam express.

George had attended Georgia Tech for four years and in his spare time had sung baritone for the Atlanta Opera Group, starring in Puccini's *Madama Butterfly* and other productions. In his senior year, he decided to change his major from physics to business management, which required two more terms of work. The decision turned out to have unforeseen consequences; because he did not graduate with his class, his draft board scooped him up and plunked him down again in Fort Jackson.

At first, the Army was a bit of a game, an intellectual challenge to George. The inherent absurdity of basic training, with its useless work and superrigid regimentation, appealed to his curiosity. He could observe it as a fascinating social phenomenon while laughing at its rigors and its humiliations, believing, ultimately, that he could outsmart it.

George's less sophisticated peers in basic training shrugged their shoulders and said they couldn't fight it. George, however, had learned how to deal with bureaucracy. With a little research, he found out that if he applied to be a conscientious objector while in the Army, he had to be given a temporary CO status until the application had been processed. That meant weeks of red tape, and meanwhile, he was not required to pick up a gun. Exempt from target and bayonet practice, George set about carving out a comfortable niche for himself.

College had taught him a lot about how to manipulate authority figures. He was not intimidated by them, nor did he outwardly fight them. In his school, unlike John's, strategy, not obedience, had been the most important thing to learn. He was cooperative with his sergeants, appeared eager to please them, and eventually talked his way into a job in front of a typewriter in the administration building.

It was not long, however, before the game turned menacing. The Army imposed no physical punishment on George, who spent a good deal of time at sedentary tasks, but it did begin to play havoc with his mind, especially when he watched target practice.

It was the seeming innocence of it all. Like the antiper-sonnel bomblets American pilots dropped that were disguised as tropical fruit. The buddy system, teamwork, team spirit. It was just like being a boy scout or a high school clubber except that you weren't teaming up to win a ball game or pitch a tent; you were teaming up to learn how to kill.

George's application for CO status was refused. He knew that even if he could land himself a desk job, he would be part of the war machine, as much a passenger on the cemetery express as the man in the front lines. He knew that the Army was more powerful than all his mental maneuvers, stronger than all the strings he could pull. It could make a corpse of a man in less than sixteen weeks, from "I do" to "Rest in Peace." So, well before those sixteen weeks were up, he left his typewriter for Sweden.

George was one of the first deserters, arriving on a snowy day in February, 1968; the trip had not been difficult for him since he had a valid U.S. passport and friends who helped him in Munich. Hans Goran Franck saw that he got asylum and found him a place in a Swedish home. He had little trouble collecting weekly checks from the Social Bureau, for he made a friend there, a tiny old lady who thought all American deserters brave and noble and always welcomed him with a smile.

George spent many private hours brooding, trying to make sense of what his grand act of protest meant to his life. There was a negative side. He had broken with his past; he had no money, no real friends. He had canceled out all the opportunities that had been laid before him. He had plummeted from a rising young man with background and status in Atlanta to a castaway whose very survival depended on the charity of a foreign government.

But there was also a positive side. He was beginning again, at an existential zero. His being was no longer entrapped and limited by the definitions of his past; he had broken out of the social slot that had been carefully constructed for him. No one expected anything of him any longer. His life was now stripped of actualities and full of potentialities. He could make it anything he wanted to make it, for he, not his parents, not the Army, but *he* was responsible for his world. In Sartre's words, he was "condemned to be free." His real self was pure possibility.

With that in mind, George set out to make some responsible decisions. He gained entrance into Stockholm University, which was made easier because of his credits from Georgia Tech, and he moved into a student room. His changed reality seemed to dictate that he abandon science and business in favor of a study of philosophy. Later he was to get the equivalent of a master's degree in the subject and earn his keep by teaching conversational English to Swedish students. He took things carefully and slowly. First, he just concentrated on how he would get through one day; then he planned in weeks, and eventually he was able to see his way through to the end of three-month intervals. Maybe, he thought, he could one day plan in years.

7
Barn Raising

As America once opened its arms with pride to the tired and the poor from Europe, so did Sweden welcome the influx of U.S. military refugees with a flush of humanitarian zeal and purpose.

The homeless Americans were golden boys, to everyone from the parliamentarian who spoke eloquently of their odysseys to the lowly welfare clerk who treated them as top priority. In time, however, the novelty wore off. The machinery which had been accelerated to ensure that Sweden's new charges got everything they needed, slowed down to the indifferent grinding pace of bureaucracy.

The first deserters to arrive had seen the birch leaves appear in the spring of 1968. By the time they had turned yellow, the exile community, quite simply, was being ignored. Applications for asylum were taking months and months, with deserters having no right to work during the interval. When the right to remain was finally granted, it was only a temporary permit which had to be renewed every three months, with the bureaucrats in a position to refuse or delay renewal arbitrarily.

The deserters were hit hard with the realization that they had no real rights, no protection against possible deportation. The outside danger temporarily dissolved petty disputes and divisions within. The ADC, the Railroad, and deserters who had previously lived in private worlds, shying from active political involvement, rallied to the cause of securing a stable environment for themselves. The exiles had to let people know they existed; a major campaign was launched to call attention, both in Sweden and abroad, to their plight.

In the States at that time, the peace movement had taken a large lateral step. Draft resistance and mass demonstrations were no longer regarded as the only forms of antiwar activity. In the beginning, the university-oriented peace leaders had infused the movement with an atmosphere of respectability—peaceful sit-ins, draft card burnings, and civil disobedience in the best American tradition by people who were willing to take the consequences of jail or exile rather than participate in the war machine.

But by November of 1968, after twenty-seven GI prisoners at the Presidio stockade in San Francisco mutinied over the shooting in the back of a fellow inmate, it had been recognized that there were other ways to break the camel's back. Attention was focused on those who had already entered the war machine and wanted to get out of it. Resistance inside the Army, on-base GI organizing, and desertion were recognized as valid and effective protests against the war.

In September, 1968, a delegation of young movement

groups from the States, including representatives of Students for a Democratic Society, made a fact-finding mission to Sweden to meet the deserters and give them a show of solidarity. They were followed in late October by a delegation of churchmen and older liberal figures, including Harvey Cox of Harvard Divinity School, and John Wilson, an early southern civil rights leader. The visits gave the deserter community an official status and an international standing in the movement.

The ADC was made an official chapter of the SDS, which pledged to begin a campaign at home to inform the American public about the community. A formal statement of support was penned by the folk heroes of the movement: Tom Hayden, David Dellinger, Noam Chomsky, Bernadine Dohrn.

The statement declared that the emergence of the deserters had given an international direction to the antiwar struggle and represented "an affirmation of the values for which the American movement is fighting at home. In your work, we see a parallel to our own struggle. The courage to stand by convictions, the determination to assert one's humanity when called upon to perform inhuman acts against other people, and the willingness to translate that stand into political action. . . ."

The ADC, born in shaky isolation oceans away from the fortresses of America, was openly proud of being welcomed into the fold of the American peace movement.

"The American deserter's committee is now recognized as an integral part of the American left," proclaimed an editorial in the December issue of the *Second Front Review*. "The ADC is now an autonomous chapter of American SDS."

And it added, a bit cockily, "The reasons behind these

developments are twofold. First of all, because the ADC is largely made up of members of the working class, we are in a unique position because we have the knowledge and experience to reach American workers. This information is vital to the American left because the working class must be analyzed and won over before a radical social change can come about."

Secondly, the editorial said, the deserters were the best ones on the left to promote resistance inside the military: "Because we in the ADC are ex-soldiers, we know how the soldier can be reached. We can give valuable insight into how the average American soldier thinks because we know the pressures he lives under and the world he lives in."

In the campaign to win public approval and support, the minds of the exiles turned toward home. Although some did not like to admit they cared, probably the single most important wish lingering in the heart of the deserter was someday to win over the older generation who disapproved so violently of him. The December, 1968, issue of the *Second Front Review* was filled with open letters home. One deserter had written to *Look* magazine, another to his hometown newspaper; a deserter named Harry Evans wrote a letter headed "Dear Mom and Dad," which said in part:

> I haven't written because I wasn't sure I had done the right thing. I know now that it was not only the right course to follow but my moral duty to do so. I miss you all and wish that I could come home just for a day or two but I can't. I shall someday if it takes ten years. But first I have to do what I can for the Vietnamese people and to change our country too.
>
> I will enclose one of our anti-war newspapers for you to

read or burn as you see fit. I know you will read it and I hope you will believe it, for it is the truth. You don't get much of that in the states, but if you permit, I will send you all that we have and let you decide for yourself.

I have learned a lot of things in the short time I've been here. I've even learned to spell a little better. I look at the facts from all sides, make a decision and stick to what I think is the truth. Most of all I learned to respect the truth at any cost, even life itself.

John Picciano, who had been haunted by the face of the lieutenant colonel who had belittled his reasons for wanting to leave the Army, wrote the man a long, sardonic letter, which was also published in the magazine.

Dear Sir:

I am writing you this letter to let you know that I did think it over and clearly understood what you told me one year ago when I was under your command.

As I remember then, I was one of your problem trainees in E4/3, undergoing basic training. I had made two unsuccessful attempts to leave the service. . . . I was summoned to your office after I had seen my commanding officer about my refusal to do any work and you took the time to have a father-to-son talk with me. You told me then that if I persisted in my unwillingness to conform that you would be forced to send me to the stockade for six months and guarantee a dishonorable discharge with a minimum of five years in a Federal prison. You also gave me a day off duty to see a chaplain and to think it over. This part of thinking it over is the object of my writing this letter to you, sir.

. . . I firmly believe that the war in Vietnam is an act of genocide committed by the present American government against the people of Vietnam and that the hogging of wealth by a few in the U.S.A. is the source of the problem. In hogging this wealth they must extract from underdeveloped countries, by force of arms and suppression, sorely needed natural wealth which is necessary for their very existence, that is, to maintain a high standard of living in the U.S.A. On the other hand, the American people, common working people, that is, must sacrifice their lives to maintain this system which benefits those few mentioned. I believe that if this small group were removed, then the war would come to an end and the American people could still live well but without bloodshed; I believe that the Vietnamese people can also progress, under the progressive government of the N.L.F., and attain an equally high standard. . . .

. . . I could not continue my association with the army and deserted on Sept 19, 1967. I am now celebrating my first anniversary. . . . Here, I am very happy and satisfied and hope you feel the same there, even though we are on opposite sides, but because I consider you an intelligent man I know you will find out your mistake, correct it and work within the army for its destruction.

Thank you for your time.

Tack sa mycket för er tid.

Sincerely yours,
x-E1 John Picciano Jr.
or better known to you as US51980146

Mark Shapiro included in the same issue some reflections on his tour in Vietnam. He talked of flying out to Tokyo after the Tet offensive earlier that year, ostensibly on leave, but in reality to seek aid to desert. Shapiro wrote:

The Tan Son Nhut Air Force Base in Saigon was full of long gray boxes. They were filled with young men, nineteen, twenty, twenty-one years old, who had breathed their last. These people did not even have a chance to find out that the war was wrong. . . . The sides of the runways were full of the caskets. They had piled up due to the three week siege when all air traffic was stopped. They tried to hide them from the eyes of incoming replacements, but they did a poor job due to the number.

The visit of American movement figures spearheaded a publicity campaign across Sweden in support of the deserters. The primary issue was political asylum. Hitherto, the government had given only *de facto* asylum, officially granting them the right to live and work in Sweden for "humanitarian reasons." The clause offered them no bill of rights, no promises on how long they could stay.

The case of Warren Hammerman, a draft refuser from Baltimore who was threatened with deportation, pointed up to the exile community the need for political asylum, a status granted refugees from Hungary and Czechoslovakia which guaranteed them permanent domicile in Sweden. The Swedish government had refused Hammerman's application on the grounds that he was a draft resister, not a deserter from the U.S. armed forces. Since he was in no immediate danger of being sent to Vietnam, the government said, he had no need for asylum. The ADC countered by holding up George Carrano, who had been accepted early on in spite of being a draft dodger, as a precedent. If they did it then, the ADC argued, why not now? Politically, the government's move to deport Hammerman was an attempt to ward off a feared onslaught of draft resisters—much greater in number at the time than deserters—into Sweden. Officials looked with dread at the example of Canada, which at that point had absorbed some 10,000 American refugees, all of whom needed housing and jobs already in short supply for Canadians.

While the ADC leaders hoped to extract from the

government a guarantee against deportation for deserters, it did not seriously expect to receive political asylum. They knew Sweden would not jeopardize its already precarious diplomatic relations with the United States further by formally putting its dissidents in the same class with those from the communist countries; indeed, the government kept insisting that its acceptance of deserters was "not an unfriendly gesture to the U.S." The issue, however, was a convenient rallying point for a host of other more urgent grievances that had surfaced with the waning of the deserters' novel appeal and their slide to the position of second-class citizens. Good jobs were impossible to find; those went to Swedes. The deserters got the dishwashing and janitorial work reserved for the Yugoslavs, Italians, and other immigrant labor. It was considered a plum if a deserter got a license to drive a taxi. The housing crisis had also steadily worsened with some men constantly moving from place to place, living out of duffel bags. Work permits were a hassle. Like residence permits, they were temporary and took months to get. Others never came through at all. Since they were retroactive to the time of application, some expired within days after they were received.

The deserters felt as if they were dealing with a bureaucracy in the throes of chaos. They asked that a special liaison officer be appointed—which immigrant nationalities often had—who would act as a link between the government and the deserters and quicken the wheels of progress. Also high in priority was a request for special language training programs geared to Americans so that they could have a chance of getting good jobs.

John had personally felt the weight of bureaucratic indifference. While staying at the Anderssons', he had lived on unemployment benefits. After returning from Bulgaria in August, however, he decided it was time for him to strike out on his own. He bid the Anderssons good-bye and took a room at the home of a Swedish youth, a teacher, in the industrial town of Solna, outside Stockholm.

He applied for a permit to work, which, naturally, was not forthcoming. Living on his own was expensive and so he was forced to get a job illegally in a brewery outside Stockholm. He kept watch over the delivery trucks to see that no bottles were broken.

More challenging was the feverish work John did during the political asylum campaign. An *ad hoc* group, Swedish Friends of the ADC, was formed to spread the word about the deserters' accomplishments, and the community began publishing the *Second Front Review* in Swedish to get their point of view across to the people. They even made a film featuring themselves called *Deserter USA*. With the help of the FNL, which acted as a publicity agent, the deserters traveled from one end of Sweden to the other—to Jönköping, Växjö, Norrköping, Lund, Malmö, Sandviken, and other cities—for speaking tours and rallies.

A twelve-man ADC delegation, including John, was sent to Denmark to lay the groundwork for a possible deserter colony there which was especially important if the situation in Sweden deteriorated. A member of the government had been quoted as saying Denmark might welcome deserters even though it was a member country of the North Atlantic Treaty Organization. In an attempt to whip up support for such a move among the Danish people, the ADC group held open information sessions at universities and civic halls, answering questions about desertion as an alternative for U.S. servicemen destined for

Vietnam. They also spoke out against Denmark's participation in NATO and urged Danish left groups to campaign for its withdrawal.

The asylum campaign peaked during Sweden's annual Vietnam Week with a mass meeting in Stockholm in which John gave an off-the-wall speech—a moving personal history laced with anecdotes and bits of politics and philosophy—which won him a rousing ovation from the 600-strong audience. The highlight of the evening, however, was the appearance of America's enemy in battle—the National Liberation Front of South Vietnam. Tran Van Hue, an NLF official, spoke as a friend of the deserters.

> . . . The Vietnamese people do not want to see young Americans being killed in Vietnam. Thousands of American lives and billions of dollars should have been used for the welfare of the American people instead of making a war from which the U.S. government has nothing to gain but unpopularity and condemnation throughout the world.
>
> The Vietnamese people highly appreciate the desertion of the American GI's wherever it might happen, in the U.S., Japan, West Germany, or in South Vietnam. The National Front for Liberation has applied lenient measures towards the GI's captured by the Liberation Armed Forces, and so far it has set free a number of U.S. prisoners of war.
>
> By their courageous acts the deserters spare their own blood, lessen the anxieties of their families and at the same time show their conscientious will not to fight an immoral and despicable war.
>
> Final Victory is certainly ours!

The Swedish public responded well to the campaign. The Jerum Affair had boosted the credibility of the deserters in general and had confirmed that U.S. military agents were indeed at work trying to disrupt the exile movement. Stockholm's three major newspapers ran editorials in support of deserters and mass-circulation magazines published in-depth interviews with several of them. Sympathetic parliamentarians argued the deserters' case in the Riksdag.

The Social Democratic government, which enjoyed the reputation of being one of the most humane and progressive in the Western world, finally gave in under the barrage of publicity. Warren Hammerman was allowed to stay and Sweden was officially open to draft resisters as well as deserters. Renewed efforts to help the community adapt were pledged.

On February 21, 1969, the Ministry of the Interior issued a communiqué which, while not granting the deserters political asylum, guaranteed they would not be deported unless they committed "grave crimes." According to the document:

> . . . deserters and other persons who refuse to take part in war activities have the possibility to safely remain in our country. As a result of special adaptation efforts, conditions are being created for them to adapt themselves and to earn their living here. Against this background it will be of no real importance to them that they, in accordance with a long and firm practice in Sweden, will not be regarded as political refugees when the Aliens' Act is applied only on account of their desertion or their refusal to take part in war activities.

It was a compromise but still a victory for the American Deserters Committee. Sweden had given in to just about all the ADC's demands without getting into more diplomatic hot water. It had held fast to its "long and firm practice" of describing as political refugees only those who had committed political crimes in the communist definition—teaching banned literature or speaking out against the state.

Moreover, the ADC got a liaison officer. The government established an Immigration and Naturalization Board and installed a Swedish social worker, Mrs. Kristina Nystrom, to interpret and act on the needs of the deserter community. The move turned out to be a godsend. Mrs. Nystrom, a sensitive, soft-spoken woman, who had long honey-colored hair and a thin frame, had lived in America and understood the American mind. She gave more than practical aid and material succor to the community. She gained the trust of the deserters, became a big sister to many, and constantly spoke up for them. She worked well beyond office hours, talking with someone who was depressed or fetching the man who missed a job interview or forgot to pick up an unemployment check.

Mrs. Nystrom took the place of Anne-Marie Rubin, an FNL member who had made a full-time job of counseling the deserters. Anne-Marie had been particularly interested in Vietnam veterans hooked on drugs and devoted her time to listening to anguished talks of LSD and amphetamine trips, helping men get into hospitals and then rehabilitation programs. Finally, however, her highly involving job took its toll and she was forced to abandon it. Mrs. Nystrom also ended up paying steep emotional costs. Like Anne-Marie, she became too attached to the handful of very down-and-out deserters who clung to her like a life raft. After two years at her job, she found that in trying to pull lost men out of stormy waters, she was being swept down into the maelstrom herself.

After the February communiqué, the bureaucratic

wrinkles in residence and work permits were finally ironed out and a consistent procedure for entry was established. Shortly after arriving, a man would file an application and present himself at the police station armed with his military identification or 1-A draft card, plus a personal statement that he was in danger of being sent to Vietnam. As a formality he would apply for political asylum and instead receive "humanitarian" asylum. Applications would take about a month to be approved and then the applicant would receive an alien's passport and both work and residence permits, valid for six months. The first renewal would be for one year, and the second, for two years. After that a deserter was eligible for permanent residence status and after seven years he was allowed to apply for citizenship.

The deserters reaped additional benefits from the crash campaign to better their conditions. Sympathetic Swedish employers called the ADC office with offers to house and hire exiles. One wealthy man, son of a lumber magnate, donated a 20-acre farm complete with stream in the town of Gävle, 150 miles north of Stockholm. Fifteen to twenty deserters went up, repaired the house, planted vegetables, and started a commune. They established a warm relationship with the villagers, who helped them raise a barn. In turn, the deserters were called on to participate in other barn raisings in the area.

The ADC's reconciliation with the government suffered a slight setback when official efforts to provide better language training took on such a martial quality that the deserters experienced a sense of *déjà vu*. Soon after the February communiqué, a "language camp" was set up in the remote town of Osterbybruk northeast of Stockholm. The government labor board called in the ADC and highly recommended that deserters who were not fluent in Swedish enroll in the camp with an eye to eventual job placement. The camp was described as similar to a barracks, with the men being able to come and go freely. The ADC paled at the thought. It was assured, however, that the camp was voluntary.

Subsequently, several deserters who applied for jobs or social benefits were informed that no help would be given unless they went to the camp. The ADC responded to what they regarded as manipulation by the authorities with strong protest; its newsletter carried a cartoon depicting GI's upbraiding both American and Swedish officials. The caption read, "This is not the Presidio. This is the AMS (labor board) camp near Uppsala. Stockade prisoners organize!"

The beleaguered government gave in. The camp was made voluntary. About forty men took advantage of it over a six-month period. The ADC dubbed it "the officers' club" because its first inhabitants were AWOL military officers.

For all the furor against the government during the political asylum campaign, the deserters had to admit privately that Sweden had been more than generous with them from the beginning. The Underground Railroad felt especially guilty about the barrage of criticism leveled against the government and was opposed to pressing the particular issue of political asylum on the grounds that it was an impossible demand as well as a selfish one. "Boy, we sure know how to bite the hand that feeds us," remarked one Railroad member.

In comparison to Canada, Sweden was a cornucopia of social benefits for the refugees. The men in Montreal and Toronto and Vancouver received no special consideration from the Canadian government. As soon as they crossed the border and were made landed immigrants, they were cast out on their own. Indeed, if a draft resister or deserter was found to be on the welfare rolls, it was grounds for deportation.

The Swedish government came out looking particularly clean and magnanimous when set against the exile's own erstwhile government, which seemed to them to be coming up with more and more ways to discredit and demoralize the deserters. None of them made more of an impact than the case of Edwin Arnett, an Army private who had deserted from Cam Ranh Bay and had come to Sweden via the Soviet Union. After hearing of the deals that had been offered to deserters by agent William Russell, Arnett, highly depressed and homesick, decided to turn himself in. He hoped and expected he would be charged with the less serious offense of going AWOL, as many returned deserters had been, and get off with a few months in the stockade as per the Russell formula.

Arnett was court-martialed at Fort Dix, New Jersey, charged with desertion, sentenced to four years at hard labor, and given a dishonorable discharge. At the same time, a report from the Senate Armed Services Subcommittee on the Treatment of Military Deserters came out recommending stiffer sentences for deserters in light of the massive numbers of defections.

It was though the ghost of Russell had come back for vengeance. Arnett's misfortune—more of a tragedy, some felt, since the youth was undergoing severe emotional disturbances and needed hospital treatment—served to douse any ideas deserters had of going home to "face the music." There would clearly be no more deals with the military; the brass was out for blood now. Any remaining trust in the word of the U.S. embassy had disappeared and the community's resolve to wait out the war in exile was strengthened.

In April, 1969, the Pentagon published a study of 116 unnamed former soldiers who had deserted to Sweden. Compiled from military records and the files of the U.S. embassy in Stockholm, the study concluded that opposition to the Vietnam War motivated only a minority of the AWOL soldiers. Of the 116 cases, the report said, 56 deserted because of disciplinary problems, 39 defected because of opposition to the war, and there were no known reasons for the remaining 21.

The study was splashed in newspapers across the United States and caused a furor in Sweden. It took an Episcopal minister named Father Thomas Hayes, who had come to establish what he called a "parish out of bounds" for the deserter community, to dissect the Pentagon study and set the record straight. He had been sent to Stockholm in early 1969 by an interfaith organization called Clergy and Laymen Concerned About Vietnam (CALCAV).

Hayes examined the report point by point and did some research into it. Among his findings were that of the 56 "disciplinary" cases mentioned by the Pentagon, 38 were charged only with being AWOL, the very offense that led to the study. Only 18 men—or 15 percent—were alleged to have committed more serious offenses. Nine were charged with drug use, mostly marijuana, 6 with running away from debts, and 8 were convicted of stealing money. Hayes also pointed out the fallacy in the Pentagon's conclusion that the "disciplinary" cases were not motivated by opposition to the war. How could the Army determine men's motivation? Hayes asked. Did their commanding officers ask them why they were deserting as they left their bases?

An official report released by the Naturalization and Immigration Board the following November also helped offset the Pentagon study. According to the report, out of 294 deserters interviewed by Mrs. Nystrom, 104 were in jobs and 103 had entered Swedish language schools. There were 7 in high schools, 9 in adult schools, 6 in vocational training schools, 26 in universities, and 14 in the language camp at Osterbybruk. Thus, more than 90 percent had adjusted in healthy ways to their difficult situation. The board also characterized the criminality rate among the deserters as very low, 22 having served jail terms, all but 2 of them for drug use.

In June, 1969, the Pentagon released another report which, ironically, gave aid and comfort to the exile community. The House Appropriations Subcommittee was supplied with detailed information on the rising rate of desertion in the armed forces. In the year ending June, 1968, there were 155,536 incidences of AWOL and 53,352 desertions (those gone over thirty days), the report said. It was news to the deserters in Sweden, at that time numbering about 300; they were part of a much greater movement than they thought. Although Sweden had been the first and for a while practically the only place an American deserter could live openly, it was obviously now only the tip of the iceberg. The Pentagon figures confirmed that there were deserters living in Canada, hiding underground in the United States, and probably in other countries all over the world. There were apparently thousands everywhere.

8

Midnight Sun

The 1969 spring brought apple blossoms, ice floes, and a spirit of restlessness to the exile community. The light came forth once again like a sweet transparent wine. Everyone was spent after a frenetic winter of political activity and ready for a change. The February communiqué had diffused the momentum of the American Deserters Committee. Michael Vale had tired of the lack of privacy—he always had a dozen or more deserters crawling out of his walls—and the widespread criticism of his militant attitudes had gotten to him. Explaining that he was "burned out," he packed up and left for England. The Underground Railroad had run off the track—collapsing for lack of support, its staunch individualism having been able to affect only a limited number of individuals.

Deserters started drifting away from the ADC, realizing that they had been too dependent on one another, that it was time to step back, reflect, and find their own souls.

Many sought counsel from Father Hayes and his family, whose home replaced Vale's as a kind of priory. CAL-CAV, which as early as 1965 had put various projects into action to help end American involvement in Indochina, had dispatched Hayes, a jovial, bearded intellectual, on a mission of "reconciliation." Hayes not only brought substantial funds from CALCAV to the community, but bore sorely needed spiritual aid as well. Hayes worked out of a tiny oblong office on a cobbled street in Stockholm's Old Town. He was a mender of fences, an ombudsman who settled disputes within the community, a father confessor, a salvager of lives, his humanity and compassion never allowing him to neglect a cry for help, no matter what time of night or day. He had brought Tootsie Rolls and Baby Ruth bars over from the States to give what he called "a little bite of America to the boys." He liked to refer to himself as helping the deserters carry a cruel burden and he called his ministry in Sweden the "flesh and bones" of his religious commitment.

Mark Shapiro and John had traveled around together for nearly a year, catching the ferry to Finland on a Friday so they could play the one-arm bandits on the boat and pick up girls in Helsinki. Mark, however, had finally brought over his Roman Catholic girlfriend from home and after long debate they decided to emigrate to Canada. Virginia's parents were opposed to their marriage because of Mark's situation and the religious differences and the couple decided it would be easier to persuade them if they were closer to home. Mark left in July and later, after marrying Virginia, entered the University of Waterloo, fulfilling the dream of a college education that he had mused about with John so often during their early months of exile.

With Mark preparing to leave and the ADC trimmed

back to a few closely knit protégés of Vale, it was easier for John to also make the break and embark on new paths. He had to have a period of reevaluation, some time on his own. Living for so many months under the tutelage of Michael Vale, he had got a crash course in radical politics. He had learned a lot but the things he learned of value were not confined to rhetoric and slogans—all the labels that reminded him of the animals in Orwell's *Animal Farm*. His radicalization was more personal and had taken place over a long period of time, beginning with the day he arrived at Fort Dix. He could look back on his life, his society, and remember with pain the injustices, big and small.

The Army had simply been a caricature of that society. The class ranking system, the brainwashing, the preeminence of one single plan for living and the intolerance for any departure from that plan, the dispatching of grunts to do the killing and the mopping up while the officers planned strategy and ate in clubs. The Army was just a little America within the big one, with its own hospitals, its own buyers and suppliers, its own laws, its own courts, its own jails.

John felt that he had not just deserted the Army, he had fled from the whole system that spawned him. When he had hightailed it out of Fort Dix and across the McGuire Air Force Field, he was not just running away from something, he was also running *toward* something else. Now here he was in a land that was not the richest or the most powerful land in the world. And yet every one of its people, no matter how poor, had free health care and the chance for a university education. Its working people lived better than his family had lived. He remembered when he was a child and his grandmother had fallen ill. To pay for her doctor and hospital bills, his mother had fed them meatless pasta and made over their old clothes. He remembered his father coming home at night from the factory, too tired to talk, too ground down by boredom to do much but turn the knob of the television set. And yet his father told him America was the greatest country on earth, anybody could be anything he wanted in America. His poor father. Never in all his years no matter how hard he worked would he walk into the factory in a white shirt and blue suit, pass the assembly line, and sit down in a swivel chair in an air-conditioned office.

John knew that his running, in part, was a search for something else, a life that could offer him more than eight hours a day bent over a pile of nuts and bolts and a game of pool on Friday night. Everyone talked about the American dream, the boy who wrestled and muscled his way up from the garbage-strewn streets to the golden boulevards. The myth said everyone had that chance. Yet if everyone succeeded, there would not be enough gold to go around. So rising up for the small people was made hard, indeed, impossible for all but the most brash and brilliant. Sometimes even brilliance wasn't enough. No matter how hard you worked, the good things always seemed to go to the privileged few. It was a revelation when he had realized that the system was really a system, that it was fixed and immutable. It was not an accident; it was part of the social dynamic—some people got most of everything and the others got little or nothing. Some were ordered to war; some were not.

The system worked well. He remembered how it worked, subtly, imperceptibly. He had seen the boys who had their college educations paid for, the ones whose desires were just one banker's check away from fulfillment. They had those little gestures of refinement, the upward tilt of the chin, the squaring of the shoulders, the little signals that they only needed to show for a second to get the job or the girl they wanted. They were the ones who would go to Vietnam as lieutenants—if they had to go—go even if it meant killing, and then, when they came back, they would take up their careers and try to forget the war.

Even if John had barreled in and tried to be like the wrestling, muscling boy of the myth, he didn't think he would have the stomach for it. As much as he wanted to climb the ladder to a better life, he did not want it enough to step on other people the way his kind had been stepped on. He did not want to kill for it.

In January, 1969, John's six-month work permit had finally come through—predated to August 13, the date he had applied. Angry, he quickly hustled a job at a bookbinding factory near his room in Solna to utilize the one remaining month on the permit before he would have to begin the process of applying and waiting all over again. The job—tying up parcels of books from 7 A.M. to 4 P.M.—paid well, $2.36 per hour. "Not bad," wrote his father. "It's more than you got here." The factory managers kept him on illegally an extra three weeks so he was able to hoard away a modest nest egg.

John's landlord was a Swedish teacher named Jorgen Lindholm, who had himself refused to serve in the Swedish Army. Lindholm encouraged him to apply for entry into a language school so he could perfect his rudimentary Swedish. In February John enrolled in a full-time eight-week course for Czechs, Italians, Yugoslavs, and other immigrants, passed it, and enrolled in higher level programs. At the end of six months he had become fluent.

John's relatives, meanwhile, had been keeping up a faithful correspondence with him. His cousins wrote telling him about the new fads in the States—the big football games, what his friends were doing. They all were concerned about the fact that he had been granted a residence permit and asked anxiously whether he was going to give up his American citizenship. His father would write frequently, complaining that John never told them enough details about what he was doing. "Why don't you come over and find out for yourself?" John replied in a letter.

John Picciano, Sr., decided to take him up on the offer. He got enough money together and took his first trip out of the United States since he made the journey from Italy as a child. John Sr. had grappled for a year with what had happened to John, trying to make sense of it all. Somehow he needed very much to see his son again.

It was a happy reunion. John borrowed a mattress for his father to sleep on in his room. The two saw the sights of Stockholm and John Sr. was amazed. His image of Europe was built from his childhood memories; he remembered only poverty, times when parents slept in the same bed with their youngest child. He was surprised to find John living on a spotless street, full of modern clean buildings, and well-dressed people.

"I never thought it was this good," he said during a tour of Sweden's subway system, which looked like a museum of modern art, each station decorated by a different artist. One stop, Östermalmstorg, had a peace mural: while the mortar was still wet, Swedish artists had written "peace" in different languages with their fingers.

The two had long talks and John tried to explain in depth the reasons for his desertion, his feelings about the war and his country. John Sr. tried to persuade him to come home.

"We could get a good lawyer, one of those from New York. You could get off lightly, maybe," he said.

"Dad, the military has its own laws. The officers try you. It's not a jury of your peers."

"Oh, yeah, that's right," replied his father sadly. He had never been in uniform, nor had he paid much attention to his country's postwar Army.

"But there's gotta be a way."

"There's no way, Dad. No way."

John's old family, the Anderssons, invited the two to a cocktail party at their ranch home in Skälby. John Sr. was a bit bewildered and awed by the rich, brightly colored Scandinavian furnishings, the cheese and nut balls impaled on toothpicks. He drifted off into a corner from time to time and nursed a glass of white wine while others were on their fourth whiskey. An American news executive, a neighbor of the Anderssons who had known John, struck up a conversation with him.

"You must be happy to see your son after so long."

"It's been good to see that he's living all right," said John Sr., glad for the opportunity to talk about the only subject which was occupying his mind. "It's reassured me. You know my wife's been very upset about all this. Her health is getting bad. You can imagine all sorts of things when your child is so far away. But I think he's going to be all right. He won't come home, but I understand more now and I think he'll be okay."

After spending two weeks with his son, John Sr. went home to Lodi, bearing good tidings. He was able to ease his wife's worry about John's welfare and that was the next best thing to bringing him home. All they could do now, he told her, was to wait and hope.

John, like many of the deserters who had moved away from the ADC that year to venture out on their own, was struck with the foreignness of Sweden. He had not really stopped to notice it before, being so wrapped up with other Americans. But his father's visit had been surrounded with nostalgia; it brought back memories of his workbench and carpenter's tools, of hamburgers and football games. He underwent a kind of delayed culture shock; although plunked in the middle of Sweden, he felt miles away from the people he mixed with day in and day out.

The Swedes were a cold people. Basically a country of farmers until this century, the nation's urban dwellers were shy and provincial as well. They were unaccustomed to striking up a conversation with a stranger and an American's gregariousness clashed with their inbuilt reserve. Many a deserter tried to begin a conversation on a bus or in a café only to get a hostile stare, as if to say "Don't touch me." It was often said that the Swedes, like Greta Garbo, really did "want to be alone."

Language erected a barrier between the American and the Swede. Working with an all-Swedish labor force was a lonely experience. During his jobs at the brewery and the book factory, John could converse with his fellow workers only on a superficial level. In spite of the fact he was fluent in the language, he could not understand the ethnic in jokes, the national sense of humor, the things that were funny only to a Swede. He would sit at the lunch table, smiling and nodding at stories the significance of which he hadn't really caught. The Swedes didn't laugh at his jokes either.

The more they lived in Sweden, the less the Americans understood the nature of its inhabitants. It was a nation run on the free enterprise system; a small percentage of its citizens owned most of the wealth. Yet Stockholm was a people's city, full of recreational facilities, youth clubs, and a free cultural center where anyone, rich or poor, could go into a booth and listen to any kind of music or lounge on a couch with coffee. Concerts and plays were inexpensive, folk groups performed in the tunnelbana, and one whole street, Drottninggaten, was reserved for pedestrians only.

Many of the rules of the land had a kind of wackiness. Speeding was largely overlooked by traffic cops, but if you crossed the street on a "don't walk," you could get a 15 kronor ($3) fine. It was legal to hold mass demonstrations, but posters announcing such demonstrations, unless posted in limited allotted spaces, were illegal. There was a 300 kronor fine (about $60) if you were caught letting your dog run loose. Etiquette had its funny quirks. Restaurants were equipped with washbasins which sat like water fountains in the middle of the dining rooms; Swedes considered it ill-mannered to eat a sandwich with anything but a fork, and to suck on a piece of ice was unforgivable.

An often-heard comment among the deserters was that the Swedish government was more intelligent and progressive than the people it governed. Alcoholism and suicide were serious national problems. The older generation was at bottom as conservative and careful as any small-town population in America. As one deserter described it, they were like Miss Frost in J. P. Donleavy's *The Ginger Man,* who wanted to cover up her navel while in bed with her lover. They were private people, slightly dull and predictable, afraid of anything new and strange.

Following the lead of their government, they registered themselves as against the Vietnam War, but that did not mean that the mass of average, straight-thinking, short-haired Swedes were ready to accept with equanimity the straggle of Afghan-coated, shaggy-maned American war refugees that kept popping up on their buses and shopping plazas. Hippiedom had not come to Sweden when the deserters arrived and even the most radical FNL-ers were not educated in all the counterculture trappings. Many an old lady would jump up when the unfamiliar hippielike figure of an American sat down next to her. Sometimes a tippler would reel up to a deserter and shout, "Yankee go home!" and a few deserters were even ejected from taxicabs, the driver screeching on his brakes when he looked back and saw the scruffy passenger.

The average Swede was rather xenophobic. His attitude toward poor immigrants was narrow, having so recently come out of poverty himself. Foreigners were immediately put on the bottom of the list when it came to getting hired, and the deserters were no exception. Many employers were doubly biased when they found out the applicant was not only an American, but an armed forces deserter to boot. One exile who was a practiced computer analyst could not get a job anywhere, although his skills were in demand, and another, a high school teacher, ended up on the streets because he was considered "too political" to educate Swedish children the way they were accustomed to being educated.

After his father's visit, John had made a decision to try to go to school. He wanted to aim for the Swedish equivalent of a college degree. The thought excited him. With an education, he could do a lot more things. It would be a new beginning for him. Perhaps he could teach in Sweden and then, someday, if the war ended, he might be able to go home. He would be going home having accomplished something, with a piece of paper in his hand that would mean a whole different life for him. He was hungry to learn. He wanted to study history and economics, to understand how the American system came to be, how one could change it. He and Mark had often discussed their long-range futures and agreed that although for now their actions had put them outside the system as quasi-revolutionaries, the only way real change could come to America was slowly, from within.

So, in September, 1969, he began a long struggle to gain admission into Sweden's halls of higher learning. It wasn't easy. The universities were highly advanced and the general rule was that an American had to have two years of college to gain entrance. He could go to Swedish secondary school to gain the necessary credits, but it was unlikely that he could pass the courses unless he was so expert in Swedish that he could grasp the terminology of algebra and chemistry. It was shades of the military. A kind of *Catch-22;* you can get into school if you have an education.

John determined to give it a try anyway. He enrolled in a secondary school in September, signing up for English literature, French, world history, Swedish philosophy, and math. The English was a breeze and the history and philosophy gave him little trouble; he could squeak by in French taught in Swedish, but the math was his downfall. No math; no matriculation. After six weeks, knowing he could never pass it, he dropped out.

The next step was a petition. Together with a few other deserters who had only high school diplomas, John prevailed upon the University of Uppsala to give them special consideration. The group all had good high school records, and if they were granted admission, the petition said, they would be willing to do extra work to make up their missing credits. The university rejected it.

Meanwhile, John went looking for a job. Having had experience in a grocery store in Lodi, he applied to the main office of the Konsum supermarkets in Stockholm. The manager told him there was a position for him as clerk at one branch in the newly built suburb of Vallingby. The personnel officer at the branch, however, talked with him for a few moments and then excused herself, explaining that she had to check with the store manager. John saw the two conferring through the glass door and overheard her say she thought John was an *avhoppare*—a Swedish word for defector. Almost all young Americans in Sweden were either students or deserters. She returned to say that there were no more openings. John went back to the main office, which put in an angry call to the Vallingby branch, and John ended up padding back to be welcomed with a smile and news that a new position at the store had just opened up.

John worked there for about two weeks. Then the manager called him in and explained that there were many Swedes in line for his job who knew more about meats. He would write John a good recommendation, but he would have to go.

"There is nothing wrong with your work," said the manager. "But this is Sweden, you know. People like you must not only be able to speak our language and do the work, you must know as much about it as a Swede."

John was at the point where he knew he would have to begin hustling. Unemployment checks were barely enough to scrape by on, certainly not enough to build a savings account with. It was of pressing importance that he get a savings account; he was tired of existing hand to mouth and he had ideas of getting together enough money eventually to pay for courses at a special American school or at least to buy textbooks to study on his own.

He wasn't very good at hustling. A lot of the exiles had made a special art of it: talking their way into odd jobs, living off girlfriends, peddling drugs, busking in the streets with guitars and a hat at their feet, sleeping on statues, collecting empty wine bottles and cashing them in. John hated the idea of all that; he was twenty-two years of age, a little old to be knocking around like a hobo.

He got work washing dishes at a restaurant in a business school in Stockholm. It seemed to him that he had gotten nowhere; he was right back where he started from after he had deserted and was forced to hustle in Vancouver behind a sink. With each dish, he became more depressed. Most of his friends had gone. Some had turned themselves in to the embassy out of desperation. Others had turned to drugs and were in jail for dealing. The ADC was just a small clique of hard liners led by Bill Jones, operating outside a damp basement office in the city; it seemed as if they were building their politics on air rather than evolving them from a life-style, from ethics and humanitarianism.

The winter came in dark, wet, and icy. He watched the students at the business school in their blue suits coming and going, carrying piles of books, laughing with one another. He felt silly in his baggy white uniform. The kitchen was hot and stank of alcohol. His co-workers were mostly Swedish drunks who would wash for a week and then leave. John had a sick sensation that he would be there forever.

As the days went by, it became harder and harder for

him to make decisions, even about the most trivial things. He couldn't make up his mind whether to wear his jacket zipped or unzipped. At night, when he put down his book and got ready to switch off the light, he couldn't decide whether to place the book even with the others or at right angles to them.

One time, on his way to the library, he walked by the train station, smelled food inside, and thought he might be hungry but he didn't know whether he ought to waste the time. He spent 30 minutes on a bench, trying to decide.

He became obsessed with neatness. He would wash a coffee cup as soon as it was dirty. He would shower three and four times a day and look for dust or dandruff on his clothes. Wrinkles on his bedspread frustrated him and he would smooth them out, and if they came back again, he would keep smoothing the spread until he got it perfect. Occasionally he would lose track of what he was saying in midsentence. Most of the time he was so tense he felt as if his neck muscles would snap.

One day it seemed impossible for him to get out of bed. He went to see a Swedish psychiatrist. The psychiatrist said he was suffering from a "real depression"—one brought on by his environment and circumstances. He gave John tranquilizers and suggested that he consider returning to the United States. John thanked him, went back to his room, and read Hermann Hesse's *Steppenwolf*. That made him even more depressed. He slept and paced, read *Catch-22*, and slept some more. He told himself he would not get out of bed until he felt he had a reason to.

The depression lasted nearly two months. It was a debilitating experience. During it, he could not see the future, he had no hope and no pleasure. Everything moved in slow motion. The days just dragged on, and he was certain that today would be just like yesterday and tomorrow would be the same. He had sunk lower than he had ever been in his life, and since he had reached the bottom, there was only one direction he could go. Slowly, gradually, he rose out of his lethargy enough so that he could see that the period of darkness had marked a major turning point in his life.

One day, he awoke feeling different. The lump in his throat was gone and the heaviness in his body had disappeared. He felt good. The sun was throwing light on the December snow and the cold, bright air swept through his window. He dressed quickly, choosing clothes without trouble, and he made another decision. He was going to get into school if he had to break down every door in Stockholm.

John made an appointment at the International Gymnasium, an expensive secondary school for foreigners. The rector was sympathetic. If John could learn French and pass a language test given to two-year students, he could be admitted to the Gymnasium and in one year, gain the necessary pre-university credits. The rector said he would probably be able to obtain a limited scholarship for John, who could work after classes to pay off the rest of the fees.

The interview infused John with enthusiasm. He found out that the quickest way to learn two years of French was to go to France, and enroll in the Alliance Française, the French Ministry of Culture's crash language school for foreigners. He wrote his parents for a loan and his father sent a check by return mail. A week before Christmas John set off for Paris.

He traveled via Amsterdam and stayed with the friend of a deserter there. A Dutch girl who was a contact for deserters making the journey from West Germany to

Sweden showed him the canals and the clubs full of international hippies.

"You know, I think you are going the wrong way," the girl said, explaining that there had been reports that France was cracking down on deserters and sending them back at the border. "You better be careful."

The warning made John slightly uneasy but he had not come all that way, using his father's hard-earned money, to turn right around again. He decided to risk it. He had no trouble getting into France, as he had a valid U.S. passport, but once inside, the news was bad. Shortly after President Georges Pompidou had come to power, the American deserters in France virtually went underground. They had been watched and harassed by police and had become fearful that this meant they were going to be picked up. Many had fled to Canada.

John got a hotel room on the Boulevard St. Michel and ate Christmas dinner alone at a little restaurant nearby. The menu was in French and since the only word he recognized on it was *fromage* he ordered an omelet.

The Alliance Française looked like a good place; the students were nice and they were pleased with the results of the training. Nevertheless, John was worried about a long stay in France. He had not realized the situation there. It was spooky. He could not imagine himself reverting to that period in Canada when he never knew from moment to moment whether he would be arrested. At least Sweden was safe; at least there he did not have to worry about being deported.

After a week in Paris, he picked up an American magazine and read that the U.S. ambassador had played badminton with a French minister, an unusual occurrence, the magazine said, and a signal that the ice was melting between the United States and France. John decided he didn't want to drown in the melting ice. He checked out of his hotel, grabbed a Frenchman and asked, *"Où est la gare?"* and caught the first train out.

Back in Sweden, he made another trip to the University of Uppsala. The admissions director was impressed by his attempts to get an education and moved by his tale of the abortive trip to France, but he was still unwilling to bend the rules. "Perhaps you could borrow some more money and get a French tutor," he said. "Do what you can, and when you've obtained your credits, we'll be glad to see you."

Once again John left Uppsala unsuccessful. But before he departed, he obtained a syllabus for a basic economics course. The list consisted of American and English books, most of which he was able to get from the library and from friends studying at Stockholm University. In early January, 1970, he settled down to spend the winter months steeping himself in the course they wouldn't let him take. He might, he thought, surprise them yet.

9
Making It

Girls, girls, girls. He loved them all. Slim, plump, soft-eyed, pug-nosed. Girls with dark satin skin. Girls who walked with a northward tilt. Czech girls, Swedish girls, English, French, and African. Girls who asked for promises of love before and those who demanded them afterward, girls who laughed at the suggestion of any promises whatsoever.

Maybe it was the times; maybe it was an awakening among Sweden's young women. Perhaps it was a kind of confidence he had gained along the way—he felt tall and full of power, his shoulders squaring. Whatever it was, they seemed to be coming to him suddenly, by the bushel. And he had an abiding desire to oblige all of them. It was a grand feeling. He knew that no matter what day of the week, he could walk out on the street and, within hours, a fair thing would be at his side.

After he returned from France, he had bought a few

good shirts, a pair of mod shoes, and a three-piece suit. Within days, he had bedded a beautiful Swedish radical. He had never dreamed how simple it was. Before, he supposed he had acted childish with women. He felt he had nothing to give them and he had been stuck in the tough defensive corner-boy routines of high school.

Sweden's much-discussed sexual liberation had seemed to be a whole mythology created by the press when the Americans came in 1968; sex appeared to be pretty well confined to the pornography shops dotting the streets of Stockholm. But for John, anyway, the myth finally became reality and once he even met a girl who wanted to make love on a train.

The Swedish radical had boosted his self-assurance. She had screamed as though she'd been stabbed and he had jumped up, asked what was the matter, and she just smiled and said, "You're good."

After a while, it all came naturally. He would be in a group and see a girl he liked and begin talking to her. As he was discoursing on Marcuse or the like, he would unobtrusively begin to finger her hair and the ice would be broken.

John liked all girls, except Americans. They were coy and prissy and giggly. Once he took an American college girl out and she played little games, tempting him and then withdrawing, pretending she was dumb when she was probably very smart. John took her back to her hotel in disgust and declined to come up for a nightcap.

For a period of several weeks, John made up for lost time. He avoided getting entangled; he saw a girl three or four times and then switched. His friends ragged him.

"What are you trying to do, Picciano, set a world's record?" said one friend.

He went after the best-looking at first, but then his fancy turned to the ones who were unusual, who were not pretty but had sexy mouths or mysterious eyes. Swedish girls offered the most challenge. The young ones, newly liberated, were demanding, and if left unsatisfied, they could be difficult. After they became attached to a man, however, they tended to follow him around like a dog, saying little and just clinging. John got bored with most of them.

In Sofia, at the International Communist Youth festival, he had had a short but very fine relationship with a Ceylonese delegate—the most beautiful girl he had ever seen, and the nicest. They would sip coffee in his room and talk way into the night. She listened to him with rapt attention and they shared ideas and laughter. At the end, she had left him a gift—two packs of cigarettes and a little note saying she would not forget their meeting and that he had meant something special to her.

By the spring of 1970 John had finished reading all the books on the economics syllabus. He had read the main books twice and quizzed himself on the important theories. They whetted his appetite and he wanted more. He had been a diligent student, making his money in the morning, reading in the afternoon and evening, and if he felt he had accomplished enough, he would have a few beers with a girl later at night. He had got a rent-free room from a wealthy Swedish friend and three or four days a week he would go down to the docks early in the morning and help load the boats or line up at the labor office at 7 A.M. for one-day jobs.

It was a good existence. Rising in the brisk morning, he would watch the play of sun and shadow and the northern light that was like no other light on earth. He loved the docks, the smell of fish and foamy water, the coming back to his room, the mountain of books on his floor and desk. He loved to drink the strong steaming Scandinavian coffee while he steeped himself in his studies.

John prevailed upon George Carrano, who was studying at Uppsala University's Institute of Economic History in Stockholm, to see if he could find a professor who could test him on the material he had read. George arranged an interview for him with a Swedish Marxist historian, who was impressed enough with John's initiative to offer to help him get enrolled in some kind of economics program. After going through several channels, the professor convinced the university's director of studies to give John an examination on basic economic theory and method.

John passed with the highest possible mark. The professor recommended John to the Faculty of Social Sciences at Uppsala, asking that he be given a special dispensation to study there, since he had proved he could grasp the particular discipline as well as a student who had studied French and fulfilled the other pre-university requirements.

Within weeks, word came from Uppsala. John had been accepted. He was expected at the university any day. It was a victory that left him grinning for days. He packed up his books, his clothes, and set off for the small, historic university town two hours north of Stockholm. It was a May morning in 1970 and he was about to walk into a life he had only watched from a distance before.

10
Children of Darkness

Uppsala University is the Harvard of Sweden. One of the oldest in Europe, the campus is a sprawling blend of stone edifices and modern architecture of sweeping glass and steel. There is an easy, convivial feel about the community of young men and women trudging to and fro between classes, pelting each other with snowballs, gathering in quaint dim-lighted restaurants to discuss Strindberg and Nietzsche around heavy wooden tables. The town of Uppsala is peaceful and charming, full of statues and steps leading down to uneven alleys where artists and sandal-makers work out of low-ceilinged stucco hideaways.

John registered as a nonmatriculated student, on probation to undertake a special study of economic history. Under Sweden's educational subsidy program, he was given a grant which covered his living expenses and room and board in a student dormitory. It was hard for him to believe that he was finally getting the chance to do exactly what he wanted to do. As he decorated his student room, putting on his own touches, building a bookcase for his reference books, hanging up pictures and quotations above his desk, he felt he was putting down roots. It was a relief to escape from the hassles of survival, the uncertainty, the displacement, the punishment of trying to hustle a living in Stockholm. He felt as if there were a place for him now.

John joined a social club called Stockholm Nation for students from the Stockholm area. He dated intelligent girls, went to plays and lectures, built up a circle of Swedish friends, and lived a thoroughly stable life. He took to his classes immediately. The lectures and the reading material were in English and he had little trouble keeping up. He took seminars on the North Atlantic community and on the industrialization of India and the British influence on the subcontinent's economy. But his favorite course was American economic history. He became particularly interested in the growth of monopolies and the antitrust laws. He read Samuelson and Keynes. He passed his probationary period with good reports and his special dispensation was renewed.

Toward the beginning of summer, John met a Swedish high school teacher named Lena Rodius. Lena was a tall, slender girl in her late twenties who was lively and cheery as a robin. She wasn't very interested in politics, but she enjoyed talking about philosophy and literature. Being older, she was more sophisticated and steadier than the young Swedish girls John had dated earlier and found to be whimsical and immature. She was good for John and he for her. He shared more confidences with her than he had with any other person and gradually they developed a secure relationship that they knew would last for some time. They spent the summer months taking long walks, cooking up elaborate meals together, and playing chess.

John's life by that time had become remote from the deserter community in Stockholm, which had undergone many changes during the first half of 1970. Michael Vale had appeared once again, descending like a thunderbolt on what was left of the ADC to convince its members to disband. The deserters were dead as a movement, he said, and political emphasis had shifted to on-base GI organizing, where all available funds were needed. Vale stayed in Stockholm long enough to dissolve the ADC formally and then he was off to bases in Germany.

With the old, highly political ADC gone, a new service-oriented one was born, geared to aiding the some 700 to 800 deserters who had by then made their homes in Sweden. With funds from CALCAV, a recreational facility called the Center was established where deserters could meet, play chess, and watch television. The center sponsored study groups and distributed maps of Stockholm and lists of shops where new deserters could get cheap clothes, food, bicycles, and other paraphernalia.

Political activity took an upsurge in the fall, however, when the community was threatened with the first deportation to the United States of an American deserter. Joseph Parra, a twenty-one-year-old Chicano from Texas, who deserted from Vietnam, had spent seventeen months in jail for drug peddling. A few weeks before his sentence was up, Sweden announced that he would be put on a plane for New York immediately upon his release.

The announcement was the culmination of several months of controversy and publicity in the Swedish press about the prevalence of drug dealing among the deserters. In April, the Interior Ministry had released figures showing that a total of fifty-three deserters had been charged with or convicted of drug offenses. The newspapers followed with a barrage of sensational headlines: DESERTERS SELLING DRUGS TO SWEDISH YOUTH and AMERICANS LEAD NARCOTIC SUBCULTURE. There were editorials depicting them as the main suppliers of LSD and other strong drugs on the mushrooming black market in Sweden. One magazine questioned why Sweden was using taxpayers' money to support "criminals." Another said, "If we accepted them so they would not have to kill in Vietnam, why are we allowing them to kill our children?"

During 1970, Sweden had expelled several deserters because of drug offenses, which the government deemed "grave crimes," while classifying stealing and assault as less serious nondeportable offenses. Until Parra's case, however, it had given the condemned men an out—a few weeks before their scheduled deportation they had given them prison leaves so they had the chance to hop a boat to Canada or leave for another country. Most of them were forced to go elsewhere via the underground since there was virtually no country that would accept an American deserter convicted on a drug charge.

Parra had taken his "escape leave" to marry a Swedish girl in the hopes it would save him from deportation. Not only did the Swedish government fail to consider that sufficient reason for him to remain, but it refused to give him a second leave.

Mass demonstrations were quickly organized. The ADC once again began a campaign for political asylum in hopes of staving off the precedent-setting deportation. In prison, meanwhile, Parra tried twice to take his life. Deserters Rob Argento and Des Carragher, who had replaced Kristina Nystrom when she gave up her job as government liaison officer to the community, appealed to Swedish immigration officials to give Parra another chance and to consider the alternative of rehabilitating instead of deporting deserters with drug problems. The Immigration Board, however, said there were not enough rehabilitation facilities for Swedish people, let alone deserters.

The appeals and demonstrations culminated in a hunger strike in a Stockholm church hall. Some fifty deserters and sympathizers camped out with mattresses and blankets for eight days, taking nothing but water. One deserter refused both food and water and at the end was taken to the hospital.

The strike had no effect. Last-minute efforts by Argento and Carragher to find an East European country that would accept Parra failed. On November 25, 1970, handcuffed and silent, he was taken to Arlanda airport outside Stockholm and deported. The government said that the Parra case had set down a principle for handling of similar cases in the future and that a dozen other American GI's serving jail terms on drug charges would also be expelled.

The government was true to its word and other deportations followed. In one case, Argento, Carragher, and other community leaders secretly negotiated with the Algerian embassy to accept a black deserter, Magnus Mitchell, who had been convicted of amphetamine dealing. After weeks of consultations, Algeria came through with an answer: It would be willing to give Mitchell asylum if he could get into the country underground but would not be willing to accept him formally and publicly right off an SAS flight. Since Mitchell was to be deported upon his release, without leave, the offer was worthless.

The deserters called Black Panther Eldridge Cleaver, living in exile in Algiers, and tried to convince him to speak to the Algerian government on Mitchell's behalf. Cleaver, however, refused to twist any arms and Mitchell was sent back to the United States.

The press stories that blamed deserters for bringing LSD to Sweden were exaggerated. The fact was that LSD had come of its own accord. Although the soft-drug subculture had begun in America in the mid-sixties, it had soon become internationalized. And it was inevitable that some of the Americans would be at the center of that culture when it came to Sweden, not only because they had access to American military channels where drugs flowed freely, but also because they often had little choice. For some deserters dealing was the easiest way to keep alive. For others it was the only alternative to suicide.

Exile took heavy tolls on all but the most stable; some started down a spiral and never came up. The spiral usually began about one year into exile. After months of washing dishes and hustling for money, a realization came to them that their brothers back home were getting married, having kids, furthering their careers, while they were standing still. Instead of trying to face themselves, choose new goals and new life plans, they became cynical. Some got caught in what was commonly called the "ripoff mentality." They collected from several unemployment offices at once, using different names. They constantly talked about "ripping off" for money American reporters who wanted interviews. They deliberately did badly on the first day of a job they were sent to by the labor board so they could get fired and collect unemployment. If they got money from a sympathetic Swede, they didn't call it charity; they said they had "ripped him off." Deep down, they came to have little respect for themselves and little respect for the society which was sheltering them. They didn't want to make a go of Sweden; they preferred to remain in limbo.

Drugs were usually a final step. The center for drug dealing—and drug taking—in Stockholm was an avant-garde youth center called Gamla Bro. It was a labyrinth of tunnel-like cellar rooms painted bright pink, blue, and lime green, where Swedish young people and American deserters sat on the floor passing around clay pipes full of marijuana to the cacophonic sounds of a flute and a piano that was played by whoever got there first. There were girls in see-through blouses, youths who yowled musically to the piano playing. On one wall a sign painted in heavy swirls read GOD OCH GLAD—good and happy. Green hashish from Morocco was passed furtively in matchboxes in exchange for 20 kronors (about $4). Arrangements for deals of LSD and amphetamines were also made. The police were aware of what went on in Gamla Bro.; it was the government's way of concentrating the drug problem. Every few nights the police would descend, looking for the big dealers and arresting a few users in the process. Usually a warning went out about twenty minutes before the raid, long enough for them to smoke up all the hash and stash away anything else. But sometimes there was no warning at all and a deserter, having lived for months in a constant state of paranoia about going back home in handcuffs, would be picked up and his fate sealed. Perhaps that was what he had secretly wanted anyway.

Others, like Jerry Dass, never went on drugs but took a different path to destruction. A Malaysian orphan, Jerry had wandered the world as a youth, ending up in California where he decided he wanted to be a *real American* and join the Green Berets. With the help of Senator George

Murphy, and a sergeant-major at the Lakewood, California recruiting station, Jerry was accepted by the Special Forces despite his status as a homeless alien. Jerry fought in Vietnam with the Green Berets and won three bronze stars and a purple heart. After participating in one too many search-and-destroy missions, he deserted to Stockholm in 1968. Jerry did well in Sweden; he lived in Uppsala, studied Chinese, his ninth language, at the university and managed a restaurant with a Swedish entrepreneur. After two years of exile, however, he saw no end to American involvement in Indochina and no hope for his return home. One day he poured gasoline over his body and set fire to himself in front of his apartment building in Uppsala. His friends ran out and tried to smother the flames, but it was too late.

For John, there were no words to describe Jerry's death. Jerry had lived nearby and had been his friend. Just when it looked as if a bright, good man were making it, he had fallen. John knew that Jerry had been upset about President Nixon's invasion of Cambodia and the Kent State shootings. John had been depressed by those events also. They meant that the war would go on that much longer and amnesty, if there would ever be such a thing, was that much farther away.

John tried not to think too much about it all. Thinking too much about the war, exile, amnesty, home, the future meant ending up like Jerry Dass. John tried to keep it all in a small corner of his mind and occupy himself with matters that were immediate, problems that had the possibility of solution. He had to step back and make assessments, examine each action, each decision, as though he were looking at himself in time-lapse photography. He had to be sure he was making the right move; otherwise, that feeling of just drifting, of being in limbo would return and reality might slip from under him like sand.

A few months after he began his studies, John decided to supplement them with night courses in French and a few other subjects at an adult school in Uppsala so he could acquire his pre-university credits. Although he was a nonmatriculated student, he could still eventually get a degree if he made up those credits.

He also took a course in industrial carpentry, hankering to augment the discipline his mind was receiving with some exercise for his hands. It was also a chance to learn a second skill to fall back on in case he could not put his studies in economics to use immediately.

In the summer of 1970 John's parents made plans to come over to visit him. The trip was much discussed among the Picciano relatives. Was Constance Picciano strong enough? John's absence had taken its toll. She would often cry at the reminders of him: a picture on the mantle, the living room bookcase he built, a neighbor calling to ask about him. The priest at St. Joseph's had been a comfort to her; sometimes she went to mass every day. She would destroy or put away John's letters after reading them, because it upset her too much if they were around the house. Moreover, she had never been on an airplane. The trip would be difficult, she knew, but in the end she decided no matter what the emotional cost, she would endure it. She had not seen her only son in almost three years.

John was delighted when he heard they were coming, although a bit worried what his mother's reaction would be when they met. Would she break down? Would she weep and plead with him to return? What would she think of Lena? He had been the center of his mother's life for so long and then suddenly he had been gone. He wondered how she would take the reunion.

John had worried needlessly. The Piccianos arrived in July and his mother treated him as though they had been apart for a few weeks of summer vacation. There were no scenes, no tears. She just smiled and embraced him. For several days, they all smiled, just sitting together in his room, catching up on the years apart. They liked Lena and were pleased and surprised at what he had done in Sweden, going from demonstrations at the U.S. embassy and speech-making to the quiet life of a student at a big university.

"I wonder if you'd stayed at home, what you would be doing now," said his father. "Maybe you wouldn't be in school."

John heard all the news about his old friends. The Cucuo twins were living near Lodi. One worked in an insurance company and the other in an A&P. Ken Barry was still living at home but he kept talking about wanting to take a trip to Sweden to see John. Sammy White, who had been at Fort Dix the same time as John, had been sent to Vietnam as a communications technician and had not seen combat. He was now a volunteer bartender at the American Legion in Lodi.

"They all ask about you," said his father. "You know, when you come home, they won't hold it against you. Ken envys you—he's never seen Europe."

Lena and John took the Piccianos around Uppsala and Stockholm. They ate at a few good restaurants, toured cathedrals, and his mother did some shopping. The subject of his future was dealt with discreetly. Once his father brought out a newspaper clipping he had saved which said there was unemployment in Sweden and men who had received doctorates were being forced to work as janitors.

His mother gently pressed him to consider coming home, but after some long talks, she said she accepted why he could not. She would rather see him free in Sweden than home in prison. For the first time, she indicated that she understood better why he had deserted. She and John Sr. had learned more about the war since then and they now felt it was a bad war. They just wished that he had chosen another method of opposing it, some way that wouldn't have put oceans between them.

As John watched them board the plane, he marveled at how different they looked from what he had remembered. He had had one image of them and now he had another. They looked older, more like people than parents. Perhaps, he thought, it was that he was more a person than a child.

After they left, Lena and he decided to live together. It was common in Sweden and carried no stigma; indeed, it was more or less accepted in young circles as a first step before marriage. They found a two-room apartment and decorated it; John bought a tape recorder, a radio, and a pair of skis.

They had many things in common. Lena was going through her own struggle in furthering a professional career. Because education was so easy to get in Sweden, teachers were plentiful and positions were hard to come by. Lena had been forced, between teaching jobs, to get work proofreading. She warned John that he would face the same problems when he completed his education. A degree in Sweden was not a passport to the fine life. John, however, was more concerned about the present and the stability and satisfaction which his studies afforded him. He had made a rule not to look too far ahead at any one time.

He did not know what the future would hold for the two of them. He could not offer Lena much. As long as he was in exile, he could never promise to provide for her, never guarantee that he could take care of the children they might have. It didn't seem to matter to her. Security was built one day at a time, she said, and she wanted to spend many more days with him.

11
Others

While some deserters sank into a world of drugs and ripoffs at different times during their exile, there were as many who rose well above their situations to become as successful and content as any young Swede. The best health food restaurant in Stockholm was started by two deserters. Immaculate and furnished with mats and low tables, the place drew its staff from deserters and their wives who spent all day every day shredding carrots, baking whole wheat bread and brewing Mu tea. Free meals were given out to needy exiles and the restaurant still managed to make a profit. Another deserter became proficient at a potter's wheel, crafted delicately designed bowls and coffee mugs, and sold them commercially. A few exiles went as far away from civilization as they could—up to the snowbound villages of Lapland in northern Sweden to chop wood and learn native crafts. Rob Argento of the American Exile Project, a government-sponsored program to aid deserters, lived happily with his Swedish wife on a farm south of Stockholm, growing vegetables and raising small animals.

The exile community had more than its share of musicians. Several bands cropped up in different parts of the country at different times. The most famous all-deserter rock group was the Red, White, and Blues. The band, started by two guitarists, a drummer, and an organist with borrowed equipment and borrowed money, grew in 1969 and 1970 until it was one of Sweden's most popular touring groups. It did the folk-rock musical *Hair* on tour and won rave reviews.

The community also yielded poets and writers. One of the most successful poetry groups was started by an Episcopal priest, Barry Winningham, who served for two years as pastor to the American exile community with funds from the National Council of Churches. The group, formed in 1970, met weekly to discuss their work and held readings at the Stockholm Museum of Modern Art and other public institutions. Much of the poetry was political and provided a platform for unexpressed feelings, for anger which had been festering inside a long time. Some of it simply reflected what it was like living in Sweden as an exile.

One member of the group, Parker Smith, a college graduate from Washington, D.C., saw his banishment as a chance to fulfill some goals his family had set for him. The last thing his mother said to him when he left, was that he get his doctorate while he was away. So Parker set out to become a Phi Delta Deserter. He enrolled in the University of Stockholm, wrote a long, dry sociology thesis statistically documenting the treatment of deserters in the Swedish press, and then dropped out, finding his own goals were really very different. He got a job with the Swedish subway system and wrote such poems as this one, entitled "Me and My Orlon":

Everyone in Sweden has an Äkta Bisam
And I've got my Orlon.
I don't know how it happened, but
    that's just the way it is
It was the middle of winter one year and
A shop owner threatened me with
"Brain Inflammation," he said
I was scared, I really was, and broke, of course.
Then he said, "69 krowns it'll be"
And I said, "right I'll think about it"
And as I walked out the door I said wow,
Right, wow, I'll think about it and it was
Cold that day, as it gets in Sweden
The tears were freezing my eyelashes
And I started thinking about that
Red Brain
"Fatal it can be," he said
And I thought, the Wily Swedes, and
Listening to the Natives, that's all
Good Stuff
And I said, "69 krowns," and that's what it was
"That's not bad, that's not bad at all"
Of course, I found out the next year
I could have got one for 38, but
I didn't know that then
And the department stores were all sold out, so
What could I do??
Of course, I didn't know anything about hats
So how could I know that everyone in Sweden has
An Äkta Bisam
And this crook was passing me an Orlon??
And, of course, I thought the silver looked nice, too
I like grey, and silver is pretty close to grey,

But, I hadn't noticed, of course,
   that everyone else had
A Brown one
And they Stared at people with Silver Ones
Like I said, I didn't know all that, and
I guess that's the reason why it happened that
Way.

There were others, like George Meals, who settled into a balance of studying and political work. By 1972 George had got his Filosophie Kanditat from the University of Stockholm—the Swedish BA, almost equivalent to an American MA. He taught English to Swedish students and had become involved with a group of deserters making weekly two-hour tape recordings for representatives of the Vietcong's political organization, the Provisional Revolutionary Government. The PRG representatives, who had an office in Stockholm, sent the tapes to Vietnam, where they were broadcast by Radio Hanoi and by PRG field stations in the south.

The weekly shows, started by Michael Vale and the early ADC in 1968, encouraged GI's to desert or resist on base. One program, taped just before the 1970 Vietnamese elections which confirmed Nguyen Van Thieu in power, was called the *Thieu Bad Show*. George's voice kicked off the broadcast with the words "I'll tell you now, folks, it's going to be just thieu (that's spelled t-h-i-e-u) bad if Thieu gets elected." It included political talks, the latest pop music and jokes such as this: "Well, everyone's talking about charity balls these days in the monied upper-class circles of America. Speaking of charity balls, if you get your balls blown off in Vietnam, it won't be for charity."

After receiving his degree, George entertained

thoughts of leaving Sweden and moving on, perhaps to Egypt to join a friend of his working in an orange grove. He had built up something of a life for himself in Sweden, however, and at least he knew it was safe, which he thought traveling around would not be. He had no desire to go back to the United States, even if he could get off with a light penalty. Being a deserter with a bad discharge in post-Vietnam America, he imagined, would not be much fun. By late 1973 George had got a job as a technician in an audiovisual lab at the university and had made plans to remain in Sweden indefinitely.

Ray Jones, Sweden's first deserter who gave himself up to serve a four-month sentence in the stockade, came back to Sweden in May, 1969—this time *not* to escape the Army but to escape what he called the tyranny of freedom in America. A black GI who fled from Germany in 1967, Jones had been persuaded to return to his unit in March, 1968, by the controversial *Army Times* editor whom the deserters claimed had intimidated Jones and several others into giving themselves up.

Upon his return, Jones, accompanied by his German-born wife and two small children, said he had been offered a deal by the Army: only four months in the stockade in exchange for a statement of repentance for deserting. Army agents had intimidated him repeatedly, he said, and he had finally taken the offer because he was told that he never would be able to return if he refused.

Jones said he had been put in solitary at Fort Dix and was visited by intelligence officers who questioned him thoroughly about who did what in the American deserter community and about possible communist connections of certain deserters. Fort Dix, however, was a playground compared to what he faced when he was released and went to live in Detroit, Jones said. He was unable to get a job because of his bad conduct discharge and he and his wife constantly met with discrimination both because of his past and because of their mixed marriage and mulatto children. His mother, who lived in Pontiac, had been ostracized by her neighbors. Jones, who had studied jazz ballet before he went into the Army, ended up collecting garbage.

Sweden granted him a residence permit, and before long he had ensconced his family in a modern apartment outside Stockholm and had started up a jazz ballet class for Swedish girls at his home. He also obtained commissions to arrange fashion shows, became involved in a number of dance projects, and found schools for his children. There were still the instances of minor discrimination, the occasional stares or dropped remarks in the store or park when his family was seen together. But, as Jones put it, it was, comparatively, like the tickle of a feather.

By 1971 the number of deserters coming into Sweden had fallen off considerably and the kind of person seeking asylum had also changed. With the steady U.S. troop withdrawals from Vietnam and the war at least on the surface seeming to draw to an end, men seeking to avoid combat were no longer flooding the country. There were some new types of resisters, however, some who were not in danger of death but who deserted as a personal protest against the war and the U.S. military system. There were people like Michael Lee Bransome. Bransome and three others mutilated Selective Service records at Silver Springs, Maryland, smeared them with black paint and their own blood, and then gave themselves up for arrest. After serving seven months of a three-year sentence, Bransome escaped during a prison leave, made his way to

Canada and eventually, in the summer of 1971, to Sweden to seek asylum. After months of deliberation, Sweden, establishing a precedent, finally granted humanitarian asylum to Bransome on the grounds that his illegal actions were a nonviolent protest against Vietnam.

There were people like Ernest Hunter, a career Air Force man who deserted at the age of thirty-five, two years before his retirement and after eighteen years of tours in Europe, Africa, and Vietnam because he became obsessed with the feeling that he had wasted his life.

Ernest, a mulatto with warm, laughing green eyes, was brought up by Baptist grandparents, who never drank or smoked and taught him the Bible from beginning to end, on a farm in Alabama. He played with white kids much of the time and he never knew what the words "racial discrimination" meant until he was an adult. When he reached the age of seventeen, he left home and went to Cincinnati, Ohio, armed with a few weeks' allowance and a high school diploma, to find his fortune.

A Navy recruitment center, manned by officers with neat blue uniforms sitting behind gaudy travel posters, caught his fancy. He was too young for the Navy, they told him, but he could join the Air Force.

Ernest and the Air Force seemed to be made for each other. He did well and he loved to travel and he kept reenlisting. He was trained as a teletype operator and then worked in communications. He served in Korea during the war, volunteered for a second tour, was stationed in Japan, Italy, and Spain and earned a promotion to staff sergeant.

In 1961 Ernest was sent to Léopoldville after the Congolese rose up against Belgian rule and the U.S. Air Force was dispatched to help fly Belgians out of the country. After the Congo, he went to Libya and then to Syracuse, New York.

In 1965, Ernest was assigned to Vietnam. He met General Nguyen Cao Ky, Premier and Chief of Staff of the Air Force, and considered it one of the greatest moments of his life. He thought Ky a dedicated man of high ideals who was trying to bring to his small country a democratic way of life. He admired the influence Ky had over his men, the way he would fly with them in the old World War II planes the Americans had given South Vietnam. He thought the Vietnamese general was a man who had a lot of guts.

After six months at Tan Son Nhut air base, Ernest began to read some anti-Vietnam War literature and wonder about the U.S. role in Southeast Asia. He wondered about the military clichés—the idealistic language, the reality of the communist threat. Working in communications, he decoded secret cryptographic information which would often tell a different story from the official line.

One day he was on a bus full of GI's who had been drinking and reveling in Saigon. A few of them started to pick on the South Vietnamese driver, calling him "slopehead" and "monkey." Ernest told them to shut their mouths and they started in on him, calling him "nigger" and "boy."

Ernest began to get depressed about Vietnam, the military, his career in the Air Force. Somehow it didn't seem now all that it had seemed before. He stayed in Vietnam through 1965, watching the war escalate, seeing more and more U.S. troops coming in and the bombing of North Vietnam. He would hit the Saigon bars every night, drinking heavily, although he had been a light drinker all his life. He stopped writing home to his friends.

In February, 1966, he was reassigned to Lowry Air Force Base in Denver. For a while, things were all right for him but then in 1968, he was sent to Wiesbaden, Germany. He experienced racial discrimination there in a way he had never done before—from both his white superior officers and his white peers. He tried to shrug it off. He kept telling himself he had only two more years to go, two years and he would have served his twenty, long enough to draw 50 percent of his regular salary.

If Martin Luther King had not been assassinated, Ernest might have made it. The civil rights leader's death plunged him into a depression. Not long afterward Robert Kennedy was murdered. Ernest walked into the sergeants' club that day disbelieving. Someone asked him if he had heard the good news. Someone else said they should have shot both King and Kennedy long ago because they were both damned communists. Ernest punched him in the jaw, walked off base, and never went back.

Several weeks later he landed in Sweden. He found a place to live in a Stockholm suburb on the top floor of an old brown house which looked haunted and had a front yard full of overgrown grass, an apple tree, and a rusty flagpole. For the first year, Ernest hardly spoke to a soul. He shunned the efforts of the ADC to get him interested in political activity. He didn't want to look like a fool, running around at age thirty-five with a bunch of longhairs who called each other brother. And besides, he didn't like the way they put down America. He didn't have anything against his country. He blamed himself for being foolish enough to waste his life in an outfit which, as he had grown older and wiser, he just couldn't feel part of anymore.

For a time he washed dishes and made sandwiches in a packaged food factory. He would come home at night, get a copy of the Paris *Herald Tribune,* a half bottle of Johnnie Walker, and sit on his balcony all evening watching the apple tree and reading about America. As time went by, he came out of his isolation. He learned Swedish and landed a fairly decent job in a gas company watching temperature gauges. He found a woman friend. He still suffered from feelings of loneliness and depression, however. It was hard for him to see where he would go from here.

A young artist named Tom Horne was among the small trickle of deserters who were still coming into Sweden in 1971. Like Ernest, Tom did not leave the Army to escape being sent to Vietnam. He fled because of what combat in the war had done to his mind.

Tom, who looks like the young poet Byron with chiseled features and silken blond hair, was nineteen and painting in an attic room in New York City in 1968 when he realized the draft would eventually get him if he did not enlist first.

He was assigned to the 82d Airborne Division at Fort Bragg, North Carolina, and trained as a medic. Tom's first drill instructor told his charges during a break that his wife sold leather-bound, gold-leafed Bibles for only $60 each and hinted that anyone who bought one would have a comfortable time in basic. Tom didn't take him up on the offer. He spent most of his spare money on books about yoga and Zen Buddhism. Often, during his leaves, he would check into a hotel with a bottle of wine and a bucket of Colonel Sanders fried chicken and bone up on his Suzuki.

After training, Tom got his orders to go to Vietnam. He

received his education about the war early on. One night, he was visiting with some guards on duty at an Army compound in Binh Dinh Province when there was the sound of gunfire close by. The guard got a call from an officer at the compound headquarters; a searchlight would be projected on a certain area and the guard was to open up on anything that moved.

The light shone on a nearby ARVN compound, the guard opened fire, and two Vietnamese fell dead. They were South Vietnamese. The officer who gave the order hated the ARVN's and he later admitted he had done it to teach them a lesson. There was no investigation of the matter. It was recorded as an accident.

One of the first men that Tom treated was a private who had got a Dear John letter from home. He walked around dazed for a few minutes and then he took his M-16, put it under his chin and fired.

One time Tom's patrol came upon an old Vietnamese man on the outskirts of a free fire zone and some of the men put him up against a tree. They cocked a rifle at his head and made believe they were going to kill him. Then they let him go.

There was a lot of drug addiction—among the sergeants as well as the grunts. There was one sergeant who used to steal from Tom's medic bag. One night the sergeant emptied the Demirol and morphine from the supply closet at an aid station and filled the containers with water. The next day, when they went out on patrol, Tom discovered he was shooting up the wounded with water. The sergeant, who was jabbering to himself and wandering around aimlessly, grabbed a morphine syrette from Tom's bag and ran away. The platoon never saw him again.

The image of one Vietcong whom Tom treated was

indelibly fixed in his memory. He had a bleeding chest wound and Tom was pressing on it to stem the flow. The platoon leader told him to get up and let the man die. Tom looked at his face; he was so little and thin, but he never screamed out in pain. He just kept his lips pursed and looked up at the trees. The platoon leader took out a ball-point pen and wrote the letters *VC* on his forehead. Then they left.

At several junctures, Tom contemplated deserting. But he always stopped himself just in time. He wanted to go to the University of California, get a degree in biology, and paint. He knew it would be hard to desert from Vietnam. Most of the deserters, unless they were able to get together the money to get to Japan and then Sweden, ended up going to Thailand and selling drugs to GI's. They got into heavy drug taking themselves and lived underground, their minds slowly disintegrating.

Tom found other, quieter ways of resisting the war. Once his squad leader caught a Vietcong bathing in a lake near a Buddhist temple. They kicked him to the ground and the squad leader was laughing and asking the men what the best way to kill him would be. They could torture him or they could shoot him, drown him, stab him, or kick him to death. Tom joined in the banter and suggested that they blow up the temple because the Vietcong hated seeing that worse than death. The squad leader liked that idea; the man was tied to a tree, and explosives were set all around the temple. They watched it explode, all the artifacts, statues, and gold flying into the air. The men cheered, and when they looked around, the Vietcong had got loose and run away.

Tom went on several search-and-destroy missions in the remote villages out in the country where the peasant people cooperated with whichever side came along on a certain day. Tom often went up ahead with the scouts and would look the other way when he saw Vietcong running away after being warned by the villagers.

Once, as he was coming into a village, a boy popped from behind a tree, ran ahead and yelled a warning. Tom recognized the boy hiding behind a chair in one of the homes he searched. He opened a closet and inside there were guns and supplies. Tom just closed the door, winked at the boy and his parents who were cowering with fear in a corner, and went outside and told his squad leader there was nothing in there.

The more Tom was in Vietnam, the more he grew to hate the war and to love the countryside. He had been able to study Buddhism much more deeply by talking to the Vietnamese people and visiting their temples. He had come to love the mountains and the sky. He never had felt so peaceful as when he sat on the veranda of a Vietnamese home, smoking grass, laughing with the young girls, wrestling with the children. When he left, he felt as if he were leaving some kind of native home. He looked over the rice paddies and the rolling hills and felt a deep sadness. A small boy he had been friends with came up to him and said, "Good-bye, Number One." Tom tousled his hair and answered, "No. I'm Number Zero and someday you'll understand that."

Back in America, Tom went through Vietnam withdrawal symptoms. Everything around him made him feel sick and sad inside. The cement and the superhighways, the absence of green trees and unspoiled earth and slow-moving, laughing Asians. He was disgusted with the new television and the latest appliances and the way his parents lived in a town on Long Island, New York. He began to have little respect for the law. He got several speeding tickets and it left no impression on him. People were always looking at him warily because he was a Vietnam veteran. They would always get around to the same question: "How many of them did you really kill?"

After a thirty-day leave, Tom went back to Fort Bragg but, three days later, went home AWOL. He was finally persuaded to go back and was busted one rank. Fort Bragg was full of men who had just got back from Vietnam. They would sit around like ghosts, smoking dope, some on harder drugs. There was little discipline for those men who had come back. The Army seemed to know to leave them alone. Tom and several friends got a house in nearby Fayetteville and grew their hair. An Army intelligence car was parked down the street all the time, and when they left the house in the morning, Tom and his friends would give them the finger or a peace sign.

Tom kept missing duty, kept getting demoted until he was down to the lowest possible rank. Once Tom and a friend decided to take a spur-of-the-moment jaunt down to Florida. They lay on the beach with a loaf of bread, a bag of grass, and got burned to a crisp. Then they got into the car and drove along the beach close to the water, singing to the radio at the top of their lungs, with the spray shooting up from the tires. The salt water ruined their car and so they hitched back to the base to face mild discipline for going AWOL.

In the spring of 1971 Tom and his roommates went to Washington for the massive antiwar demonstrations leading up to May Day. Tom was fascinated with the guerrilla theater and the colorful activities. There were plastic M-16's and young Asian girls acting as dead and dying Vietnamese. There were thousands of protesters, full of rage and shouts, police coming down on them with clubs, Vietcong flags, Army helicopters flying overhead.

It was like a surrealistic version of his Vietnam days. Something came over Tom and he knew he had to take a stand, to show that he was a part of this mammoth angry defiance. He wanted to get arrested. If he could not get arrested, he thought, then he would desert. He had only one month to go before he was due to be discharged and that, to him, made it even more important that he make a sacrifice, if only to purge himself of the guilt of Vietnam.

He never went back to Fort Bragg. After the demonstrations, he hitchhiked back to his parents' home on Long Island. They were shocked to learn that he had decided to desert and could not be talked out of it. But they supported him. He lived at home for three weeks, helping his stepfather, a bricklayer, mix cement and working as an ice-cream vendor to earn enough money to leave the United States.

Tom flew to England and visited relatives in Scotland for a while and then worked his way to Göteborg, Sweden, polishing chrome and guarding crates of scotch on a cargo ship. He lived in Stockholm, studying Swedish and painting, for a year and then decided to make definite plans for the future. Unlike many deserters, Tom had some options. Although he was reared in the United States, he had relatives in England and was eligible to take up residence there, no matter what he had done in the American Army. Tom went back to England in 1972 and entered London University, where he started working to get the degree he had dreamed of getting back when he was counting off the days in Vietnam.

12

Don't You Know Me, I'm Your Native Son

In March, 1973, two months after Hanoi and Washington signed a peace accord which ended a decade of bloodshed between them, Sweden closed its doors to American war exiles. There was no reason, said the small Scandinavian nation, for it to accept young refugees from the mightiest power in the world now that this power had stopped sending its sons to war. The deserters and draft dodgers already living in the country could stay, but new ones would be turned away. As if to punctuate its declaration, Sweden halted at its border two black GI's who had deserted from West Germany and turned them over to U.S. military authorities.

It was the end of an era. Sweden had been a symbol of security and safety for Army deserters since 1967. It was the only place in Europe which ever welcomed them un-conditionally, offered them legitimacy and a chance to live openly and with dignity. It had been a historic period, and as it drew to an end, the deserter community in Sweden gradually shrank in size. What was once a swelling colony of some 700 to 800 men in the peak war years had, by the time the last bomb was dropped on Cambodia in August, 1973, dropped to an estimated 400. Some 150 had sur-rendered themselves to U.S. authorities. A few others had embarked for less secure but more hospitable climes such as France, England, and Italy. Some went to Algeria and other Arab countries cool to the United States. A few sojourned to India and Bangladesh. The bulk went to Canada, where they could be closer to family and friends.

The end of the war had taken the steam out of the American Deserters Committee in Sweden, which had been a political boiler room during 1971 and 1972. Every event in the United States which bespoke repression had aroused murderous feelings in the ADC militants. The Attica prison riots and the Christmas, 1972, bombing of Hanoi had sparked large, impassioned demonstrations, as well as a series of anti-Nixon posters which told less about Nixon than it did about the deserters and the deep abiding bitterness that exile had sown in their minds. One poster carried a large photograph of Nixon drinking a cup of coffee; only the coffee had been painted blood-red and was dripping down the sides of his mouth.

By early 1973, however, the violent reactions had abat-ed. The Vietnamese were no longer being bombed (although the Cambodians were). The last U.S. combat troops had been removed from Southeast Asia. The deserters began to think of themselves. The question of amnesty was not a new one, but it was only after the peace agreement that it became, to most of the exiles, a valid one. The debate had begun too soon. As early as 1971—two years before the war ended—amnesty was one of the most talked-about issues in the United States. The January 17, 1972, cover of *Newsweek* was emblazoned with the question: Amnesty for the War Exiles? President Nixon and Vice President Agnew were strongly opposed. Exile publications in Sweden and Canada responded to the hue and cry with demands for an unconditional amnesty, but the majority of deserters and draft dodgers did not really believe any kind of "forgetting" would come in the near future, nor did they think it should. They felt that no person who had placed himself outside his country because of a war it was waging could in good conscience think about reentering while that war was still going on.

In February, 1973, the exile community in Sweden, deciding that amnesty was no longer a premature issue, launched a campaign for repatriation. The ADC changed its name and its newsletter to *Up from Exile* to focus on the drive. It coordinated efforts with Canadian exiles and the American-based Safe Return Committee, which was working to bring deserters home, publicizing their cases, and helping get them off with light sentences. The three groups planned an all-exile conference for February 19–22 in Paris with representatives from Sweden and Canada, as well as delegates from Clergy and Laity Concerned, Vietnam Veterans Against the War, and the American Civil Liberties Union. The goal was twofold—to agree on an amnesty platform and to publicize the plight of the refugees. Seats had been booked to fly in the U.S.-based groups and Canadian exiles and other arrangements were finalized when France suddenly banned the meeting, one day before it was scheduled to begin. The French Interior Ministry said it would be "disruptive to public order" and create a bad atmosphere for the twelve-nation Foreign Ministers' conference on Vietnam slated for the following week. American embassy sources in Paris confirmed that the United States had requested the ban.

The twenty-odd representatives who had already arrived in Paris held a quiet, closed-door meeting anyway, without fanfare and without news conferences. They reached a common position calling for unconditional universal amnesty for draft resisters and deserters in exile and at large in the United States, those serving terms in American jails, and those who received less-than-honorable discharges from the military because of resistance to the war.

Back in Sweden, the organizers of Up from Exile pressed on with the campaign, giving interviews and news conferences, writing letters home to friends and Congressmen. Because of the historically negative connotations of the word "deserter"—cowardice, disloyalty, treason—they began calling themselves "self-retired veterans." John Picciano, who had been scheduled to go to the Paris conference as a delegate before it was canceled, came down to Stockholm from Uppsala to speak on behalf of the community for a CBS television spot after the return home of the POW's from Vietnam. John had, over the years, become a practiced media speaker. He was one of the few who, given three minutes to make five points, could do it concisely and thoroughly, without getting flustered. The CBS interviewer asked him if, now that the prisoners were home, he felt he should be allowed back also. Yes, he said, he missed America, he felt six years of exile had been enough of a penalty to pay, and he wanted to come home, but only if he could return as a man of conscience, not as a criminal.

Meanwhile, the campaign for a universal no-strings amnesty gained momentum at home with support groups burgeoning throughout the United States and amnesty bills of all types being submitted before Congress. The American Civil Liberties Union put its Project on Amnesty under the leadership of Henry Schwarzschild, who traveled from city to city speaking so eloquently on behalf of the exiles that even archconservative William Buckley was outdone when the two debated on Buckley's television show *Firing Line.* Clergy and Laymen Concerned started up a drive headed by former Attorney General Ramsey Clark, gold star mother Louise Ransom, and Carl Rogers, a founder of Vietnam Veterans Against the War. Mrs. Ransom, who lost a son in Vietnam, called for an amnesty because she said the name of her son "would be dishonored if we discredit these other victims of the war." Veterans of Vietnam—members of VVAW—actively demanded amnesty for deserters from the war they had served in.

Shortly after the peace accord was signed, President Nixon said he would not countenance forgiveness for the few hundred men who had resisted the draft. Angered by Nixon's interpretation of the numbers involved, the ACLU and other organizations compiled figures of those who would benefit from an amnesty, based on official sources, primarily U.S. government agencies, as of September, 1973. They fell into the following categories:

Deserters: 32,000 at large, according to the Department of Defense, living either underground in the United States or in exile abroad.

Draft Resisters: a total of 52,143. 7,443 of them were convicted by federal courts for violations of the Military Selective Service Act. 5,700 faced "outstanding" indictments for draft violations. 39,000 others were officially referred by the Army to the Department of Justice for prosecution. 30,000 to 40,000 of those at large believed living abroad, mostly in Canada. Perhaps an additional 100,000 who failed or refused to register for the draft remain liable for prosecution.

Less-Than-Honorable Discharges: 450,000, according to Department of Defense figures. Most such discharges resulted from AWOL crimes and other offenses which would not be punishable in the civilian world, such as disrespect to an officer, and carry with them severe disabilities, including loss of veteran's benefits and disqualification for civil service and other employment. The majority of the bad discharges resulted from war opposition and race-related incidents.

By late 1973 the best thing to come out of the amnesty movement was in some cases, particularly in instances of draft evasion, a kind of *de facto* amnesty. Of 3,495 draft refusal cases the government pressed in 1972, 977 were convicted and only 260 of those spent time in prison. The .chances were more than fifty-fifty a returning draft evader could get off on a technicality or if convicted, receive a suspended sentence or alternative service in hospitals or community projects. There was no guarantee, however. Prosecutors and judges varied from area to area. In Texas, for instance, many returning refusers were routinely convicted and given five-year jail terms. In Buffalo, 162 draft dodgers were indicted during a period from December, 1972, to June, 1973, alone.

The situation for deserters was even less heartening. Since 1971, a bounty of $25 had been placed on their heads. Some returnees were convicted of the lesser charge of AWOL and let off with a few months in the stockade and a bad conduct discharge. Others were charged with desertion, which carries a maximum penalty of five years at hard labor and a dishonorable discharge. Richard Bucklin, a deserter who spent five years in Sweden, returned expecting to receive an administrative discharge, but was brought before a General Court Martial instead. It often seemed a matter of chance. Either way, because of the stigmatizing discharge papers, coming home meant paying a lifelong penalty. For those like John Picciano, who had been away for a number of years and had been vocal in the exile community, the projects for a light sentence were gloomy.

For John, however, just about the next best thing happened. His parents, after sitting powerless and broken for six years, became involved in working for his return home. At Christmas, 1972, the Piccianos were approached by John's old friend George Carrano and asked to be one of the founding members of a new organization called FORA—Families of Resisters for Amnesty. George, who had recently returned from Sweden to be cleared on a technicality of draft violation charges, was working for the Safe Return Committee, which conceived FORA based on the conviction that a movement of resister families would be a powerful and influential force on Congress. George talked to the Piccianos over dinner in their tiny basement kitchen in Lodi, New Jersey. He proposed that Mr. Picciano come out and publicly tell his and his son's story.

John Sr. trusted George, for he had met him during his

visits to Sweden, but he was apprehensive about getting involved in politics. He didn't know anything about it. He didn't even know who his Congressman was. He was afraid of what the publicity would mean for his wife, Constance, who had been afflicted with arthritis and nervous tension during the years of her son's absence.

A letter from John in Sweden dispelled the elder Picciano's doubts. He called up George. "Johnny says I should do it, and if it will help get him home, I will."

FORA scheduled television and radio appearances for John Sr. and for other parents, like Abe Simon, father of Lew Simon, who had deserted to Sweden in 1969 and become a close friend of John's. At first, the elder Picciano was stage-shy and hard to draw out. But with the gentle prodding of his wife and letters from his son, he gained more confidence and it gradually became easier for him.

In May, 1973, the campaign peaked with *ad hoc* Congressional hearings co-convened by FORA and Representative Bella Abzug of New York. A panel of seven Congressmen heard the testimony of family members of thirteen resisters, including John Picciano, Sr., in the House Judiciary Committee hearing room while President Nixon entertained 600 returned POW's at the nearby White House.

John Sr., his voice shaking, read a statement written for the occasion by his son and then said his own piece quietly under the glaring television lights and the buzz of reporters.

"Johnny had to go in the Army because we didn't have the money to send him to college.

"I went to Sweden and tried to persuade him to come back, but he made me see that I was wrong.

"I support my son. I think he did the right thing. This

war should never have happened. It was wrong to send all those men over there for nothing.

"Johnny's done nothing wrong and he should be able to come home."

The last to give testimony was Mrs. Lora Sowders of Detroit, mother of eight and wife of a disabled World War II veteran. She told how her son Eddie had come home from Vietnam depressed and upset and had finally deserted. "It's the sons of poor families like mine that are bearing the brunt of American suffering in Vietnam now," she said.

Mrs. Sowders, in a move which surprised the Congressmen, ended by introducing Eddie, who had come to the hearings to conclude three years of underground life. He stood up, recited the facts of his case, his disillusionment in Vietnam, his reasons for deserting, and then went in search of police to give himself up. The thirty-odd family members present in the hearing room stood as one and applauded.

The testimony of the families gave a unique picture of what the essence of the exile problem was: parents separated from sons, dreams shattered, lives dislocated. By the end of the five-hour hearings, Representative Abzug was in tears. The other Congressmen, perhaps faced for the first time with the flesh-and-blood problems of the constituents they had not seen since they shook hands with them at the supermarket, were also touched.

Outside the conference room, Abe Simon asked his Congressman from New York, Ben Rosenthal, who had supported a conditional amnesty bill for draft dodgers only, why he thought his son, who had deserted, was a criminal. Rosenthal promised that he would rethink his position. Later that year Lew Simon was to fly in from Sweden to stage a public surrender in New York as a test case to secure better treatment for returning deserters. The Army responded harshly; it lodged a preliminary charge of desertion, rather than the AWOL, against Simon.

John Picciano, Sr., ended up paying a price for his work with FORA. Shortly after he made his first radio appearance, he and his wife started to get crank calls and letters. One caller told him he ought to be shot, whereupon John shouted back that the caller was the one who should be shot. There were a few people in the community of Lodi who abruptly stopped speaking to them.

The harassment, while initially frightening them, only convinced John and Constance of the importance of what he was doing. It was not only helping John, but also slowly and quietly giving them some peace of mind. For years they had felt helpless, at the mercy of a situation they did not understand and could do nothing about. Now they were no longer alone; they were one of some 700 Families of Resisters for Amnesty who had suffered as much as they.

"I'm doing something for Johnny now," John Sr. said, "and it's not just him. It's all the boys. We've got to bring them all back."

In the 1973 summer of Watergate, when the break-in at the Democratic Party headquarters the year before turned out to be a small part of a more widespread political sabotage scheme, the calls and letters stopped for the Piccianos. Friends who had never mentioned John's desertion dropped over to express their support. It became easier for John Sr. to talk about his son not being a criminal deserving of criminal punishment with the continuing disclosures about the illegal acts committed by Nixon administration officials.

When the prisoners of war returned from camps in North and South Vietnam in February, 1973, they were given thorough medical and psychiatric examinations. A State Department official concluded that the captives of the Vietcong, after a long period of undergoing alternating cycles of illness and health, of malaria, dysentery, and other tropical diseases, had been relatively free of severe disease. Their bodies, he said, had stabilized at a somewhat lower life-supporting plateau and they had become healthy within that framework.

So too did the exiles come to settle into a kind of half-existence. After years of ups and downs, of bouts of exhilaration and loneliness, high hopes and deep disappointment, of good jobs, bad jobs, hard study, hard-drug using, they came reluctantly to accept their fates and to live at a lower expectation level.

They heard the people back home, moved by the spectacle of the prisoners stepping pale, thin, and wounded off the U.S. Air Force planes, demand that the deserters and draft dodgers pay a price for their return also. There was no way, no words that the exiles could use to respond to that demand. Only they knew the kind of price they had already paid and would always be paying.

They had not sat chained to cages for months. They had not subsisted on a diet of rice and pork fat or suffered the humiliation of being enemy prisoners. They had not endured physical torture. But that did not mean that they had gone unpunished or that they had run off, as their detractors put it, for a "lark in Sweden" or that they had been free of the agony of alienation for even one day out of the hundreds they had been away.

Many of them were just nineteen or twenty when they deserted. None of them knew, when they made their choice, that the war would last for not one, or two, but for five more years. For those years, they had been living in a vacuum, thrown at a young age into an unnatural environment under an abnormal set of circumstances. The experience had interrupted their maturing processes and stunted the growth of many of them. When they should have been becoming adults, starting careers, building bases, discovering naturally who they were like their peers at home, they were suspended in limbo, waiting to begin. Their young energies, finding no constructive outlet, were channeled into hating the system that ostracized them, the country that rejected their values. It had been a time of deep despair. The deserters knew why Socrates had chosen death over exile.

By the fall of 1973 John Mitchell, the former Attorney General of the United States, and Maurice Stans, the former Secretary of Commerce, had been indicted for conspiracy to obstruct justice in a federal investigation of one of Nixon's top campaign contributors. Vice President Spiro T. Agnew, months after insisting on no amnesty for the "criminal" young Americans hiding out in "deserter dens," faced a grand jury inquiry and possible indictment for extortion and bribery. He pleaded no contest to a lesser charge of income tax evasion, and resigned. Presidential adviser Henry Kissinger urged "compassion" for the beleaguered administration officials under investigation for offenses related to the Watergate affair. Meanwhile, demands for President Nixon's resignation came from

220 WAITING OUT A WAR

both conservative and liberal quarters alike. The AFL-CIO mounted a campaign for impeachment.

In the midst of the governmental chaos, the amnesty debate droned on. Exile communities in Canada and Sweden, while publicly demanding an amnesty, privately were cynical about the prospects of coming home. The feeling was that a country so torn apart by the war, Watergate, and snowballing economic crises would not have the time to spend trying to solve the dilemma of the thousands outside its shores.

John Picciano tried not to think about it too much. He had been putting down some stakes in Sweden. He had almost finished his schooling and was due to graduate from the University of Uppsala in January, 1974, with the credits for a *Filosofie Kanditat*—a degree he would receive as soon as he completed the necessary pre-university courses that he had been taking in night school. He had done well at Uppsala and was thinking of studying further for his doctorate. There was little alternative for him in Sweden other than being a professional student; there was no company or institute that would employ him as a promising educated young man on the rise, no firm that would disregard his circumstances and nationality and jump him to the front of a waiting queue of Swedes. At least university life kept his mind busy.

He and Lena had drawn apart, taken separate apartments, for she had come to want marriage, and he felt he could not offer her that because for now, he was a man without a future. They were periodically close, however, and at times found happiness in the moment.

As John watched his friend Lew Simon and others take the previously unthinkable step of returning home and surrendering themslves, he would feel alternately depressed and tempted. He felt as if he were inside a leaky well with the water running out, and he wondered what would be left if it went dry . . . if one by one all the deserters went home leaving nothing behind. The thought of surrendering himself to the U.S. Army put a knot in his stomach. He didn't know how he could face the same thing he had run away from, the same stockade treatment, the same brittle-chinned, cold-eyed sergeants, after all these years. And yet, he thought how good it would be to go home, to be with his parents, to taste American beef, use pencils with erasers, watch some American television, go out among people who spoke the same language, knew and loved the same hills and rivers, read the same books and magazines. He was in a strange kind of limbo between two cultures; he was nowhere, suspended in an uneasy plane where he would alternate, for instance, between listening to the voices in an American movie and reading the Swedish subtitles. If he could be fairly sure of being discharged from the military with just a short time in the stockade, he might do it, he just might go home.

John's parents had come over to Sweden for another visit a few months after the *ad hoc* Abzug hearings; his father had been excited and proud about his work with FORA, and the two had more to talk about than ever before. Shortly after his parents left, John wrote George Carrano in New York and asked him to get a lawyer to look into his case to see if there was a chance he could get off lightly. George and FORA responded quickly to John's interest in returning by manufacturing and distributing hundreds of silver bracelets engraved with the words "Amnesty for John Picciano." He might not be ready to come home yet, John thought, but at least he knew that he had friends who cared and would help him when he was.

Sometimes John wondered what would have happened if he had just finished out the Army and gone to Vietnam or had chosen an easier way to get out of the military. He wondered what he would be doing right now. Perhaps he would never get over the deep bitterness, the feeling of having missed his youth. He would carry it around like a bell on his neck for the rest of his life. If and when he went home, he would have to explain himself over and over again. And there would always be someone who would not understand, who would secretly wonder about him.

Yet, during all this time, he knew he had become many things he would not have become otherwise. Sometimes, as the winter light played on the snow outside his window, he thought of Lodi. The long warm grass on the banks of the Saddle River where he used to sit and read . . . Pap's Luncheonette . . . the car he used to take apart . . . the girls in the school parking lot . . . the spaghetti dinners around the kitchen table . . . the smell of new wood at his father's workbench.

Perhaps, he thought, one day he would return home a Doctor of Economic History. He would not let himself hope too hard. There was a time and place for everything. Maybe one day there would be a time for dreaming again. One thing he had learned was that there were never any endings. His life in Sweden was in order, and for a while that was all that mattered.